GUIDE TO
SIGNALS &
INTERLOCKINGS

Design and build a working system for your layout

By Dave Abeles

Kalmbach
Media

On the covers:

Front: Conrail SLSE (St. Louis, Mo.,—Selkirk, N.Y.) comes east at dusk through the interlocking at CP 280, passing Onondaga Yard on its trip across central New York on author Dave Abeles' HO scale Onondaga Cutoff model railroad. *Dave Abeles*

Back: AT&SF GP60M 125 leads the hot Q-NYLA westward and is about to "knock down" (pass) the signal at East Texico, pictured on the layout, left, and on the dispatcher's screen. As the train moves across the line, the dispatcher monitors progress and clears routes, just like the prototype. *Sammy Carlile*

All photos by the author unless otherwise noted.

Kalmbach Media
21027 Crossroads Circle
Waukesha, Wisconsin 53186
www.KalmbachHobbyStore.com

Published in 2021
25 24 23 22 21   2 3 4 5 6

Manufactured in China

ISBN: 978-1-62700-825-9
EISBN: 978-1-62700-826-6

Editor: Eric White
Book Design: Lisa Schroeder

Library of Congress Control Number: 2020939300

Signal heads on the famous Norfolk & Western Blue Ridge Grade east of Roanoke, Va., are installed so as to only be able to show possible aspects through the single crossover in the interlocking. Norfolk Southern train 236 is behind Canadian National power in 2014.

Contents

Introduction...4

Chapter 1
Prototype history and development...........................7

Chapter 2
Signal system basics: knowing your options.............32

Chapter 3
Getting started with a manual signal system............54

Chapter 4
Train detection: The signal system's foundation.......64

Chapter 5
Wiring signals for your model railroad 79

Chapter 6
The interlocking and your layout 88

Chapter 7
Controlled signals for your model railroad..............102

Appendix and Bibliography...........................126

Signals can add magic to night scenes like this one at Onondaga Yard. The mounting up on the bracket mast at left ensures operators can see their aspect over the equipment in the foreground.

Introduction

A working signal system is a component of model railroads that many admire, but relatively few have accomplished. The basic trackside animation of changing aspects is prototypical, visually fascinating, and communicates to engineers and train crews the status of the track ahead. In the prototype, signals allow railroads to move more traffic with greater safety, efficiency, and capacity. In fact, from railroading's earliest days, the application of a signal system is what created what we today think of as mainline railroading.

In all signal systems, the displayed colors or positions change as trains pass or as routes are lined and cleared in order to provide safe and efficient movement of trains. These displays are called "aspects" and are a compelling part of railroading. On our model railroads, fully integrated working signals quickly catch the eye and become a defining feature of the layout, adding to the atmosphere and movement of even the humblest trains.

General Railway Signal Co. "SA" dwarf signals at control point (CP) Port Reading Junction, Manville, N.J., are lined up for a westbound move. The bottom head is flashing red, so the signal is displaying a Limited Clear aspect. Jack Trabachino

There are many questions. How exactly does this work? What do the different displays mean? How does this translate to a model railroad?

This brings us to why you're reading this book: My goal is to get you started, to help you understand the basics of railway signaling, to help you apply those basics to your railroad, and to implement a working system of your own. To be clear, there is a reason why this book is being written: signals are both costly and complicated. Signals are essentially a hobby within our hobby. Signals have their own language, and the design and construction of the system is intimidating. Even simple systems can quickly add up to a substantial cost relative to the rest of the layout. A functional system may seem insurmountable given limitations in time and resources. Given these barriers, how can we demystify signals? How can we understand signal systems to make them more approachable for more modelers?

Like most good modeling, we start with the prototype. We do, after all, have numerous examples to learn from and follow. Signaling overall is a complicated system, yet each of the parts of that system can be considered as a component of the system, a layer upon which the next layer relies. Approaching the system layer by layer will help you build an understanding of each, and we can then work to combine them into a system of signals and devices to move trains safely. We will begin with prototype basics, learn the basic terminology, think through the process of design to support train movement and operations, and finally move forward to apply those ideas to your railroad in a logical manner. Each layer can be broken down into basic, but related, elements. The layers are constructed to work together in a logical manner to display signal aspects. Design and construction of a signal system on your layout is likewise accomplished in layers that provide a path for modelers to approach signaling for the first time.

Depending on the complexity of the routes involved, traffic density (frequency), and your prototype, different approaches are available to the modeler. Signal systems range from the most basic to highly complex and automated. For example, at the simpler end, basic automatic block systems convey only the occupancy by trains of adjacent segments of track or the aspect of the next signal. More complex systems—including controlled signals and turnouts and systems for the operation of groups of signals and turnouts—have to be constructed in

Conrail BRSE crosses over in the interlocking at CP 277 around local freight WAON-10, demonstrating the flexibility of two-track CTC. Once BRSE clears, the local will get a signal to proceed west and continue its work in Fayetteville.

such a way that each signal to proceed indicates a routing aligned for safe movement with no intervening traffic or misaligned switches. Signals may be fully automatic in some of the simpler cases, but in others can be controlled locally by a tower operator or remotely by a dispatcher, or by a crew after requesting permission. To model prototypical signal systems, we focus first on the basics and how they apply to your layout. Upon that foundation, choices will be clear on how you can proceed to construct the system that is right for you and your railroad.

As our world changes with the incredible power of the internet, you can rest assured that your learning will not stop with this book. I will give you a start and get you running—and you're in good company then to build upon this foundation moving forward. In that light, I have included several bibliographies of previous books and articles explaining model railroad signaling and a list of manufacturers. Further, I suggest you search in the

Model Railroader archives online for the numerous articles on signals, signaling, and interlockings that have appeared over the years. This is a golden time in the hobby and your options have never been as accessible or unlimited.

The glossary on page 143 will help you get started. This is a generalized and high-level glossary. Individual railroads, and almost every railroad company at some point in its history, had variations on these definitions.

Acknowledgements

This book is the culmination of experience with signals while building my HO scale Conrail Onondaga Cutoff, and of a lifetime of learning about railroads and how they work. I am grateful for so many people and for this opportunity. My journey in life is forever affected by the knowledge and companionship of Jack Trabachino. As we got into the details of the construction of this layout, it was the suggestions of Al Werner and then skills of Nick Anshant for system architecture that brought the signals and CTC to life. Jack and Rich Wisneski worked to build an operation for the railroad creating a realistic, enjoyable and challenging operation for visitors, fueling my passion for the hobby and helping create the foundation for sharing it. This specific work was at the suggestion and mentoring of Tony Koester, without whose vision this writing would not have happened. I am indebted to Tony as well as mentors Jerry Dziedzic and Mark Hemphill, both of whom provided suggestions, feedback and hours of discussion as the text continued. Eric White at Kalmbach was patient and worked with me while I learned the process. In the last weeks of writing it was the skilled eyes of Mark as well as Rich, Dave Barraza, Bill Breeden, and Joe Relation that gave me invaluable proofreads. And through it all, the patience and steady strength of my wife, Kristen, and children Susie, Teddy, and Pete—they make life and home a wonderful experience, and I am grateful for them and for everyone that assisted. Any success of this work is a result of the energy of this group; any mistakes are mine alone.

A manifest freight rolls east toward a medium-approach aspect on Track 1 at dusk in East Syracuse, N.Y., during heavy snowfall on a frigid January 8, 2014. This aspect indicates that the train will enter Dewitt Yard. Searchlights are designed with lenses that focus the beam, so that the light is projected in the best possible way for crews to see signal aspects in any weather.

CHAPTER ONE

Prototype history and development

Signals have dotted the railroad landscape ever since railroaders needed to keep trains safely separated on the same track. On tens of thousands of miles of main track in the United States and Canada alone, railroad management directed its engineers, skilled craftsman, and laborers to design and install signals to communicate to crews whether their route ahead was properly aligned and clear of other trains, **1**. Understanding the basics and how those signals apply to the prototype is the most important step in constructing a signal system for your layout, **2**.

Searchlights manufactured by Western Railway Supply Co. more than 50 years ago guard the interlocking at the west end of Cima, on Union Pacific's former Los Angeles & Salt Lake main line. Signals and associated hardware are built to withstand everything from harsh winters to the heat of the Mojave Desert, as seen here.

Signals come in many different shapes and sizes, and are mounted in different ways. Here, GRS searchlights are mounted on a bridge over the Rio Grande main line through Ironton, Utah. *James Belmont*

Extra 1585 west takes coal loads through downtown Thurmond, W.Va., on Ted Pamperin's beautiful Chesapeake & Ohio. The home signal has been cleared for an eastbound as well, showing a "clear" indication.

Before signals

In the era when a railroad only ran one train at a time, there was no need for a signaling system. As soon as a railroad began to operate two trains at a time, it realized the need to keep each train movement separated—using "smoke signals" to apprise yourself of the location of the other train only goes so far on sharp curves, or in wooded terrain, or at night. To address this need, railroaders developed some basic operating principles. Each train movement required two preconditions: (1) authority to occupy the main track, (2) assurance that no other train was authorized to occupy that track—what railroaders call protection against other movements. Each of those have different requirements. There's a simple acronym that railroaders use to keep this straight:

C: Condition of the block, communicated by signal or by paper (order)
R: Representation of superior trains—paper (timetable or train order) or signal
A: Authority (signal, timetable, or train order)
P: Permission to enter block (signal, verbal, timetable, or train order)

The original authority and protection scheme was the railroad's published timetable issued to each employee: a paper document that provided for temporal separation

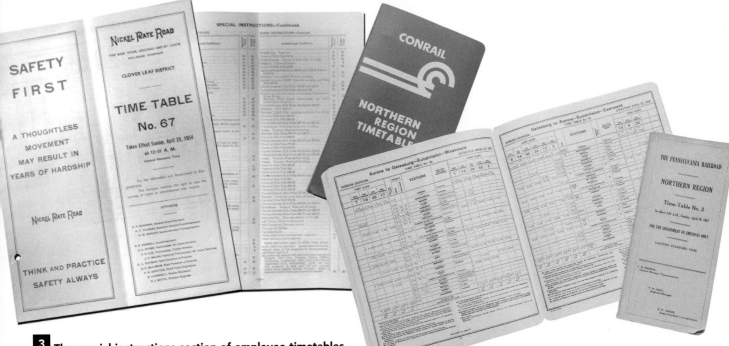

3 The special instructions section of employee timetables typically contains a wealth of information of use to modelers, including the names and locations of a wide variety of industries. *Tony Koester*

4 Timetables come in multiple formats. The Conrail timetable is a loose-leaf binder with plastic covers. The Chicago, Burlington & Quincy and Pennsylvania Railroad are bound paper. *William Zuback*

of trains, **3**. As long as a train crew abided by a document that authorized each train to proceed between defined locations at a certain time, and proscribed meeting locations and times with other trains, a train crew had both an authority to occupy a main track and proceed, and assurance that no other train would surprise it around a sharp curve, **4**.

Each train crew handled its own switches, and simply left its initial station when it was time to do so. If a train ran late, the timetable handled that eventuality too, by prohibiting an opposing train from leaving the meeting point until its counterpart arrived.

For the first few decades of North American railroading, the timetable was absolute. Only scheduled trains ran, regardless of circumstance. Each train had a published schedule. Each train would wait for an opposing train at a pre-determined spot designated in the schedule. Flagmen walked back from a train that had stopped to manually flag any following train, in order to protect the rear of their train from a following train. But if there were delays, whether mechanical or bad track, very soon all trains came to a standstill unless one of their crewmen walked forward and worked out an ad

5 This is St. Croix train order number 2 ready for delivery with a clearance card attached. The clearance here serves as a receipt or invoice showing the train crew what's being delivered.

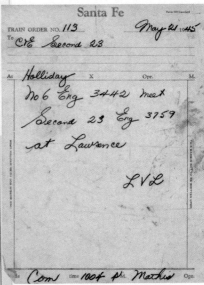

6 Here's an example of a Form S-A train order, delivered by the Santa Fe operator at Holliday, Kan., in 1945. It tells the conductor and engineer of the second section of the westbound *Grand Canyon* (No. 23) to meet the eastbound *Ranger* (No. 6) at Lawrence. The engine numbers in the body of the order help crews identify the trains they meet.

9

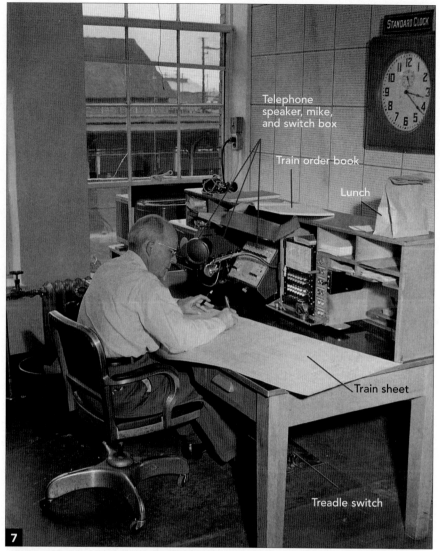

Telephone speaker, mike, and switch box

Train order book

Lunch

Train sheet

Treadle switch

7

Here's a Southern Pacific train dispatcher at Sacramento, Calif., surrounded by the tools of his trade. A model railroad dispatcher's office could re-create such a setting, including the push-to-talk foot switch. *Phillp R. Hastings*

hoc agreement with opposing trains that could enable the opposing train to advance. This wasn't really a problem when a railroad was a few tens of miles long, and only ran a few trains a day; if the track was washed out or a locomotive had failed, the other trains weren't going anywhere anyway.

But as railroads began extending and consolidating, and as scheduled trains increased from a handful a day to more than a dozen, the published timetable became by itself inadequate. And, as railroads began to become adaptive to daily and weekly variations in traffic demand, the practice of every train needing a published schedule became unwieldy.

Three solutions appeared in the 1850s: the idea of the "extra train" to accommodate one-time or intermittent increases in demand for freight services, the "extra section" to accommodate passenger demand that couldn't be accommodated on a single scheduled train, and the "train order"—a written instruction that temporarily modified the fixed times that trains ran and where trains met, for specific trains at specific locations.

These extra trains or sections would need authority and the assurance of clear track just like the scheduled trains did. In 1851, the first documented train order was written in the U.S. on a predecessor of the Erie Railroad. This document, issued under the authority

8

No. 10 races by Extra 612 West (note the white flags on the steam locomotive) in the passing track at Metcalf, Ill. Note the lack of signals; in timetable & train order operation, extras like 612 West above must clear the main line for timetable trains like No. 10. If No. 10 is late, 612 has to sit and wait. (Trains have to clear following first-class trains by the time shown at the next station to the rear.) *Tony Koester*

A long steel pipe connects the ground level actuating lever to the signal's tilting blade. Each Genesee & Wyoming crew has to stop, unlock the lever, and change the signal before using the crossing, and then reset it once the Erie's main line is clear. *Harold W. Russell*

John King has carried the idea of replicating the work of professional railroaders to an amazing degree with his "model" of a dispatcher's office. All of the communications hardware is authentic. *Paul Dolkos*

The crossing tender is changing the number of signal balls he will display to clear the route Boston & Maine engine no. 1731 will take as it passes through Whitefield, N.H., in July 1978. The brackets beneath the balls are used to hold kerosene lanterns to display night indications. *Robert Gabbey*

In the 1930s, this signal displaying two balls authorized the arrival of a Sandy River & Rangely Lakes train at Phillips, Maine. *Edward Bond*

of the railroad's superintendent, modified the published timetable and allowed a train to run outside the times listed in the timetable.

The new idea worked, and was soon expanded to other areas, and other railroads, **5**. This new "Timetable & Train Order" (TT&TO) system assigned trains a ranking of superiority based on their "right," class of train, and direction of travel. "Right," a precedence given in the timetable or superseded by written order, and "class," defined in the timetable, were provided to all trains as part of the official timetable.

Class segregated trains by importance. For example, a railroad

The vertical semaphore arm on the left, facing away from the photographer, indicates a clear manual block to an approaching Erie-Lackawanna train in Newark, N.J., on May 6, 1966. The red-painted arm indicates "stop" for trains traveling in the opposite direction. *Rich Taylor*

would commonly designate its principal passenger trains (including extra sections) as first class, its secondary passenger trains or principal freight trains as second class, its remaining scheduled trains as third class, and all other trains as extras, which had no precedence over anything.

The timetable also designated a certain direction of traffic as superior to the other direction, thereby designating which of two trains of the same class moving in opposite directions had to clear the main track for the other. Authority to move was conveyed by paper timetable or written, signed train orders only, and crews were accountable to use their paperwork and knowledge of the territory to safely move their train and perform their duties, **6.**

The dispatcher updated a "train sheet" in real time showing the location of every train on his territory as it reported in at stations, or as operators reported trains passing their stations, **7.** When the timetable needed temporary modification to enable on-time trains to advance against the schedule of a late train, or to operate multiple extra trains, or for any other condition that might impair safety or efficiency, the train dispatcher would issue a train order.

This train order reached each affected train through an intermediary, the operator, who worked at individual stations. Operators would signal

trains that they had an order for the train, and the train would either stop and sign for mandatory orders that restricted a train's timetable authority, or "pick up on the fly" orders that did not require a signature because they did not restrict the train's timetable authority.

Crews waiting for a meet would stop the train on the main or a siding as per the timetable direction, holding while other crew members aligned a route or waited for a timetable meet, **8.** Once moving, trains then stopped once again to re-align turnouts once the equipment cleared. There was—and is—plenty of waiting with TT&TO operation as each train crew waited for assigned meets and trudged back and forth along the tracks aligning switches.

While TT&TO rules worked for most railroads, and on many for more than 100 years, the system has significant limitations. Once traffic exceeds about 10 trains a day on a single track main line, it becomes unwieldy and labor-intensive. Operators were required around the clock at dozens of stations. Dispatcher workload resulted in trains waiting while the dispatcher updated his train sheet and issued new orders.

Double tracking, with trains assigned a current-of-movement on each track, minimized the number of train orders required and allowed relative fluidity of traffic as long as deviations from the published timetable were relatively few.

Manual signals

However, the growing post-Civil War economy demanded more freight and longer trains. Any railroad with traffic densities beyond around 10 trains a day—especially longer and heavier trains—on the main line needed to move traffic faster than a walking pace. Some system had to be developed to communicate to train crews from a distance, preferably without stopping, and preferably with fewer train orders.

To meet this need, various forms of signaling were tried. Early signals were called "semaphores" with a nod to the flag signals that had a long history in ocean shipping and military communications.

Sir Charles Paisley, a British major general, developed a system to adapt the marine semaphore system to other uses including the railroad. Charles Hutton Gregory installed some of the first fixed railway signals

13 Three of the many types of train-order signals are shown here: upper-quadrant semaphore on the NKP at Montmorenci, Ind. (top), searchlight at G Office on the NKP and NYC in Lafayette, Ind. (center), and a lower-quadrant semaphore at Duncan, N.C., on the old Norfolk Southern (bottom). *Tony Koester*

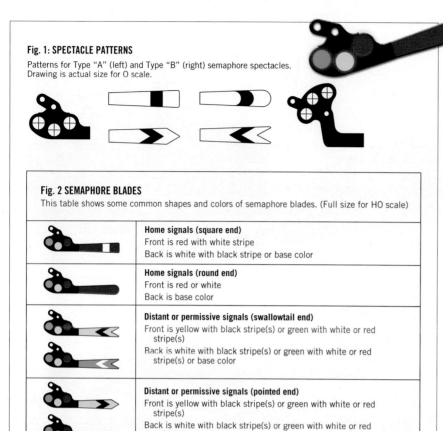

Fig. 1: SPECTACLE PATTERNS
Patterns for Type "A" (left) and Type "B" (right) semaphore spectacles. Drawing is actual size for O scale.

Fig. 2 SEMAPHORE BLADES
This table shows some common shapes and colors of semaphore blades. (Full size for HO scale)

	Home signals (square end) Front is red with white stripe Back is white with black stripe or base color
	Home signals (round end) Front is red or white Back is base color
	Distant or permissive signals (swallowtail end) Front is yellow with black stripe(s) or green with white or red stripe(s) Back is white with black stripe(s) or green with white or red stripe(s) or base color
	Distant or permissive signals (pointed end) Front is yellow with black stripe(s) or green with white or red stripe(s) Back is white with black stripe(s) or green with white or red stripe(s) or base color

14

using semaphores on the London & Croydon Railway at New Cross, a location in southeast London in 1843 where the newly enlarged junction also accommodated the South Eastern Railway. The semaphore board signals set at a horizontal position were "stop" signals, preventing equipment from running into misaligned turnout points or other equipment.

Building on British ideas, some American railroads began to install manual signals at stations or towers along the mainline route. Yards, spurs, and sidings had slow speed limits enabling train crews to simply keep an eye out and stop before a conflicting movement. Therefore, early signals applied to main tracks only.

The earliest signals were a swinging board or a ball that could be moved by rope, wire or lever, and whose position would indicate whether the track ahead was clear or not, **9**.

This was the first inception of what would become known as a manual

15

Manifest freight Q268-17 moves east at Depew, N.Y., after a snowfall in February 2016. Another movement has been lined east on Track 2, and shimmering more than a mile distant are clear aspects for both tracks.

block system, where occupancy of the main track was communicated to train crews by the operator using the position of the board or the ball. If the track ahead of a train was clear, then the operator would set the signal to show "clear" and the train could proceed.

Once the train passed the operator's tower or shanty, the operator would telegraph to the dispatcher and to the next tower operator that the train was "on sheet" (OS) past his or her location. In fact, because each operator was communicating on an open telegraph line, all operators and dispatchers on the line were able to be aware of all train movements, **10**.

Once a train was reported OS by the agent or operator on a stretch of track between two towers or stations (a "manual block"), the block would be treated as occupied with the manual signals at each end set to "stop." This signal protected the authorized movement from conflicting moves until the authorized train or equipment was reported clear of the next station along the line by the operator or agent at that station, via telegraph.

With the early ball-shaped signals, a ball moved to the highest position was the signal indicating that the block was clear, originating the term "highball" on the railroad, **11**.

This manual block system (MBS) worked well and was a huge improvement over pure TT&TO systems without signals, enabling faster train movements. But, as ever, growing mainline traffic and the need to keep bigger trains moving more quickly meant that MBS installations were pushing the limits of the possible.

Operations men were looking for an answer and this British idea of the fixed signal along the route was gaining acceptance. One step toward more efficient movement of trains was to add manual block signaling to more trackage, **12**. Manual Block Signals evolved, using not only semaphore blades but later color lights as well. On some lower-density lines these signals lasted well into the 1970s and even 1980s, **13**. But MBS systems suffer from several limitations. In terms of

General Railway Signal Co. searchlights atop the modified former New York Central signal bridge at CP 286, East Syracuse, N.Y., stand guard before dawn on May 25, 2014. *Nick Anshant*

Signal 3572 shows an "Approach" aspect, telling the crew of any eastbound to expect a red aspect at the next signal ahead on Ted Pamperin's C&O layout.

The green-over-red aspect on Track 1 at CP 431 in Depew, N.Y., signifies that the next two blocks ahead are clear of traffic. The yellow-over-red aspect on Track 2 gives warning that the next signal ahead on Track 2 is set to stop. This signal bridge also holds the three-head eastbound home signals, visible to the left, to CP 431 from both yard leads for the massive Frontier Yard to the west.

Norfolk Southern operator Jeannie Fouse records numbers from sets of helper locomotives at legendary ALTO tower in Altoona, Pa., at the base of the former Pennsylvania RR Allegheny Grade. *J. Alex Lang*

speed of movement and track capacity, they are labor-intensive and force trains to space out, even on unidirectional track—a train can get no closer than one block to the next preceding train.

Because each block stretched from station to station, or tower to tower, they were often 5 to 10 or more miles long. In addition, from a safety and protection perspective, MBS systems do not include any fail-safe device—all protection was manual.

Automatic signals

A major breakthrough for safety was found in the then-new electric relay circuits that could determine whether a track was occupied. In 1873, Dr. William Robinson designed a new system with automatic block signals, using relays and based on the electric track circuit. His patents would become origins of the Union Switch & Signal Company in decades to come. Relays include a magnet and an electro-

magnet. If both rails are attached to a power source, and there is no train in the block, the circuit is complete and the relay is energized. The wheels and axles of a passing train connect the rails, completing the circuit so that electricity flows across the wheels and axle. This "short circuits" the relay, which is then de-energized and opens.

An energized track relay is the result of current flowing through the entire length of the track circuit, which indicates the entire block is unoccupied or "clear." When any wheelset rolled onto the block, the wheelset would conduct the power between the rails, and "shunt" or short-circuit the relay. With no power, the relay would de-energize and literally "drop out" by gravity, changing the signal from clear to stop. We will discuss this in Chapter 2. Typically railroads designed their signaling systems and operating rules so that the signal displayed "permissive stop" meaning that after a stop, the movement could proceed slowly. This enabled following trains to close up behind a stopped or slow-moving train in order to expedite all trains.

If, for example, a heavy freight train bogged down on a grade, a following train instead of waiting could come up behind it, and reduce delay to the

Chesapeake & Ohio Train No. 3, the *Fast Flying Virginian* with engine 613, roars around a local freight high atop the Allegheny Mountains. This interlocking, appropriately named Allegheny on Ted Pamperin's C&O, is equipped with CTC, which makes such runaround moves simple to accomplish and very efficient.

21

All the tools of the towerman's trade are at hand while he watches the action on the Chicago, Burlington & Quincy at 6:22 p.m. Friday, Dec. 10, 1954, at Mendota, Ill. *Philip R. Hastings*

22

The Union Switch & Signal interlocking machine for ALTO interlocking in Altoona, Pa., glows with another winter night's activity in 2011. *J. Alex Lang*

following train compared to it stopping and restarting at the entrance to each signal block.

These electrically operated signals were automatic and conveyed the status of the blocks ahead and protected against following moves and crossing moves. As an additional benefit, they also protected against broken rails: a broken rail breaks the circuit, dropping power to the relay. This causes the signals on each side of a broken rail to display red.

A large flat board decorated as a semaphore affixed to a horizontal pivot mounted to the top of a pole comprised the earliest automatic signals. The semaphore rotated in a vertical plane. When it was pointing up or down, it indicated "Proceed" and when it was horizontal it indicated "Stop". Even this rotation had a fail-safe principal behind it: weights and levers affixed to each semaphore were designed so that if electrical power failed, gravity acting on the unpowered mechanism moved the semaphore to the horizontal position, **14**.

23

It's 11:08 p.m. at ALTO tower as Jeannie Fouse shuffles paperwork preparing for a westbound move. Centralized traffic control machines for ANTIS, HOMER, ROSE, and WORKS glow to her left, each of those plants remotely controlled from ALTO. *J. Alex Lang*

Semaphore installations had practical limitation. First, a movable semaphore, even an automatic or electric semaphore, has many moving parts—gears, bars, rods, and the arm itself—that required lubrication and adjustment. Second, those moving

parts could be adversely affected by snow, ice, rain and wind. Third, they required some form of lighting to be visible in the dark. This last issue led engineers to begin to include lights in the semaphore arm.

An overview of the automatic signals in mile 261 of CSX's Chicago Line, Oneida N.Y., January 2011 shows GRS pole-mounted searchlights providing distant aspects in advance of the home signals for CP 263, some 2 miles west. *Nick Anshant*

BNSF C44-9W 4769 leads another manifest freight heavy with insulated boxcars loaded with California wine toward eastern markets at Caliente, Calif., on the famed Tehachapi Pass owned by Union Pacific in April 2011. For now, legacy Southern Pacific searchlights guard the interlocking here where the railroad narrows to one track, but UP's signal upgrade has the replacements standing by, including a new bungalow.

Railroads run in all sorts of weather, and the signals are designed and maintained to handle their work in all elements. GRS searchlights shine on CSX's former Conrail, nee-NYC main line in North Syracuse, N.Y., in January 2014 during heavy lake-effect snows off nearby Lake Ontario.

The sun sets behind the bracket mast signal at CP 293 in Solvay, N.Y. While dim from this angle, the crews will see brightly lit signals thanks to the focused lenses on the searchlights.

Lake-effect snowfall surrounds the automatic signals on the bridge at MP 287 in North Syracuse, N.Y., while CSX General Electric diesels take another train of stacked containers west. Signals must be designed to work in all weather conditions, and maintenance in the United States is carefully regulated by the Federal Railroad Administration.

Adding light

When railroads advanced from a purely timetable or time interval-based operations to some form of block management system, manual at first, the term "clear" from the earliest days related to the condition of the block. In a block management system, if there are no trains in the block ahead, the block is considered to be clear of other trains. If there is a train in the block, then the block is considered occupied.

This concept remains true today. The type of signal aspect displayed at the entrance to a block to indicate that the block is clear relates only to the condition of the block ahead. Early block signals indicating "clear" could be a ball signal in the high position or semaphore signals in the vertical position.

With the advent of lighting, the first lamps were kerosene-lit. Since these were simple lantern flames, they were relatively low-intensity lights. Color at this stage was a huge technical hurdle, with some systems relying on red cloth to color the displayed aspect. Even with the invention and adaptation of early electric lights, the bulbs were low wattage by today's standards. The technology to impart color to glass was, even in the late 1800s and early

The Pennsylvania RR's famous position light signals, built by United Switch & Signal in the 1930s and 1940s, lasted until 2018 across much of the former PRR's Pittsburgh Division. Here, automatic position lights at MP 245 guide three movements at once in April of 2014.

1900s, limited, and most colored lenses significantly degraded the amount of light passing through.

For safety reasons, white or clear lenses, giving the brightest, most visible, light at the time were therefore used to indicate a clear block. Even after the development of early electric lighting, the convention remained to use the brightest light indications for clear aspects. (The rule remains to this day that a signal that is dark or not displaying any aspect must be treated

as displaying the most restrictive indication that signal can give.)

Visibility was, of course, critical to signal systems for a number of reasons. Most obviously, visibility was a key component in determining stopping distance and therefore the maximum speeds that could be allowed on any stretch of track, **15**. The greater the visibility, the greater the stopping distance so the greater the maximum speed, **16**. Visibility also became more of an issue at night or in adverse

29

Powered turnouts, such as on the Denver & Rio Grande Western, allow an operator or dispatcher at a remote location to control large areas of the railroad.
Railway Signaling, November 1929

weather. More visible was not only safer but also allowed faster trains and greater carrying capacity for each mile of signaled track.

Another approach to increasing speed and capacity was to give trains greater warning of a stop signal ahead, **17**. Therefore, the "caution" or "approach" signal came into use to slow a train if the block ahead of the next block, for example, was occupied. Instead of a hard stop, and in order

to keep trains advancing rather than sitting and waiting, a train given an approach or caution signal aspect could continue to move, but at a slower speed, and prepared to stop short of the next signal, which is presumed to be displaying "stop."

Originally, caution signals were colored green. When the automatic block signal system was developed, including a sequence of aspects, the three-signal aspect sequence

then became white, green, and red. Railroads, however, discovered that a green or red lens could break, bleach to a lighter shade, or fall out, leaving the appearance of a clear lens.

With "clear" defined as a white light, a signal displaying white because the red or green lens had broken or disappeared would create a "false clear" indication. So, eventually, white was eliminated from the primary aspects and green was substituted for "clear." Yellow was introduced for "caution" or "approach," leaving red for stop, **18**.

White signals today are still in use, but are given a bluish tint and called "lunar white" and are used to modify certain aspects in such a way that if the lunar signal is absent, safety is not compromised.

A common use of lunar aspects is for what is called a "grade signal"—a lunar is added to a signal governing uphill trains on a steep climb. When a following train comes up behind a

30

Classic Northern Pacific cantilever signal masts and GRS searchlight signals guard the interlocking at Plains, Mont., while Montana Rail Link train LAUSPO (Laurel, Mont., to Spokane, Wash.) passes. This is an example of route signaling, where the aspect is displayed for a route through the interlocking and the speed is determined by the timetable.

slow-moving uphill train, the lunar signal illuminates and enables the following train to pass a Stop and Proceed signal without stopping, reducing the risk of break-in-twos on a train restarting on a steep grade.

These new signals seemed like a lot of expense, and they were. But they allowed railroads an astonishing amount of extra capacity to more efficiently use their track to move trains. Track space is a finite resource—the slower trains move, the less capacity a track has; adding tracks is an expensive capital proposition and generates increased operating costs as well as cost to maintain the additional infrastructure, **19**.

Expensive signal systems imposed their own costs but as compared to adding double or triple track, or purchasing additional locomotives and rolling stock to make up for train delays, signal systems were almost always the more cost-effective option, **20**.

Interlockings

From a safety perspective, more, faster and heavier trains running through more complicated junctions were leading to more severe accidents in the late 1800s. Human error was a primary factor in many accidents. Public outcry for improved safety following hundreds of multiple-fatality accidents placed great pressure on railroad companies to improve safety. A mechanical solution was needed that would keep trains separated, but also allow for routes to be set ahead of time so trains could keep moving.

For junctions between railroad lines, and where two or more railroads crossed each other at grade, the next major step forward was the Saxby mechanical interlocking. John Saxby developed an early and revolutionary idea in Britain in the 1850s when he invented a new system dubbed "preliminary latch locking" that mechanically lined switches and signals so that routes through turnouts were lined safely.

This system was the first to place locking devices into the mechanism that prohibited an operator from lining conflicting routes or clearing conflicting signals. Once one route

When CTC was installed across the New York Central Water Level Route in the 1960s, the main line was reduced from four or more tracks down to two main tracks with controlled sidings. The full-width bridges remained into the 2000s, a clear juxtaposition of the change over time. *Nick Anshant*

Conrail TV-207 blasts upgrade through the interlocking at CP 277 on the Onondaga Cutoff. Formerly a four-track main line, addition of CTC in the 1950s reduced the main line to two tracks, aligned to the south side of the right of way.

was set and the signals governing entrance to that route were cleared, all conflicting routes were locked out.

Using this new system, an operator manipulated large steel or wrought iron levers that were connected by mechanical linkages to each switch and signal. The levers were arranged so that no clear or proceed signal would be displayed until all turnouts were property aligned, all signals were properly displayed, and the desired track routing was clear.

The levers were arranged so that the mechanism they controlled was locked together—was interlocked—so that conflicting routes could not be allowed. Saxby received a patent for this invention in 1856 and the innovation

A General Railway Signal Co. signal box cover plate in Toston, Mont.

was a huge success with thousands of interlocking levers in service at numerous British interlockings before 1875, and rapidly spreading through North America in the late 1800s, **21**.

In an interlocking plant, a group

33

34

Deep in the New River Gorge, classic Chesapeake & Ohio color light signals guard the interlocking in April 2014 as the rain falls on another loaded coal drag rumbling through downtown Thurmond, W.Va., like coal trains have for more than 100 years.

A unique dwarf-mast signal sits at the west end of Cima, atop Cima Hill in California in 2014. Signals come in many shapes and sizes as ordered by their home railroad and built by competing signal companies.

of levers, locks, and bars were arranged so an operator would line a desired route, lock the route into the machine, and the machine would then allow the operator to display signals for movement over that route. Simultaneously, the lock would prevent the operator from displaying signals on a second route in conflict with the first.

The machine would display stop indications on signals on all other routes and prevent the operator from changing the route until the movement was clear. This basic system, or something very like it, is behind those

pictures of rows of floor- or cabinet-mounted levers in control towers of the 1900s through the 1950s.

At least to start, the only power supplied into the system of moving levers was brute force—the strong arms of the men in the towers pulled levers which in turn moved mechanical bars, joints, and in some cases wire cables stretching from the tower to the switch points and signals. These strong arms became the genesis of the term "armstrong" or armstrong interlockings.

As interlockings became more complicated, plants evolved into

24-lever, 32-lever, or even larger installations. Because armstrong systems required manual labor to set each signal and switch, the larger installations were complicated and hard to learn.

Naturally, complication was also costly to maintain and bad weather—rain, snow, and ice—played havoc with levers, points, and rods. But the new installations sped up traffic and increased safety.

In the United States, rail traffic boomed in the 1870s after the post-war slump following the American

35

The Montana Rail Link dispatcher has lined train 840 westbound through the interlocking at Toston, Mont., on September 30, 2014. On single track, such as the case here on the former Northern Pacific main line, only one route can be lined through the interlocking at time, hence the red signal on the siding at right.

CSX trains pass at CP 431 in Depew, N.Y., east of Buffalo. Signaling large main lines required expansive bridges over multiple-track rights of way. This unique bridge has controlled signals on two yard tracks, but automatic signals on the main tracks as identified by their numberplates.

Civil War. As the limitations of purely armstrong systems became apparent, railroaders sought ways to improve performance with mechanical assistance.

Early experiments on improved mechanical systems were carried out by the New York Central & Hudson River RR (a New York Central predecessor) at Spuyten Duyvel in New York City in 1875, and the Lehigh Valley and Reading railroads experimented with an early hydro-pneumatic system in Bound Brook, New Jersey, in 1884.

Electro-mechanical systems became possible with the development of reliable electric motors. Mechanical installations replaced muscle power with powered assists so that operators could rotate smaller hand levers on a board or console instead of shoving or pulling large wooden levers standing on the floor. Refinements continued at a rapid pace and by 1900, hundreds of interlockings were in service on railroads nationwide, ranging from just one turnout in some interlockings

to several dozen in others at major junctions or the throats to large central stations in major cities, **22**.

In railroading, as in life, things are always changing. As the towers began to spring up around the nation on main lines and even secondary routes, they began to take on a life of their own. Many historians and enthusiasts will remember visiting towers, and especially so if a friendly operator gave a lineup or took time to teach the visitors about the machines. To crews, towers were a human railroader watching out for you, waving day or night to the passage of yet another train.

Model boards, on which the track layout of the interlocking was diagrammed, contained small lights— track occupancy lights (TOLs) that would illuminate when the track circuit showed occupancy. Track blocks approaching the tower from both directions had an alarm bell that would give a loud, audible chime or ring upon a train entering that block. Like so much in railroading, it seemed the tower would always be there, **23**.

Auto racks roll toward a "clear" aspect at CP 283 in Dewitt, N.Y., in January 2014. Complicated interlockings generally required more complicated signal aspects in speed-signaled design such as this plant adjacent to the former NYC Dewitt Yard.

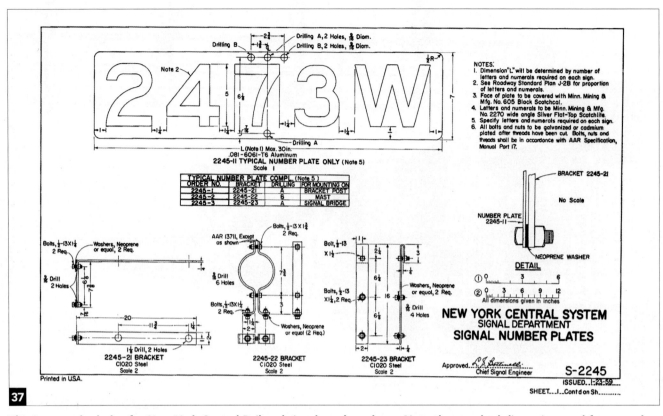

37

This is a standard plan for New York Central Railroad signal number plates. Note the standard dimensions and fonts used throughout the system. This plan also became the standard plan for Conrail systemwide.

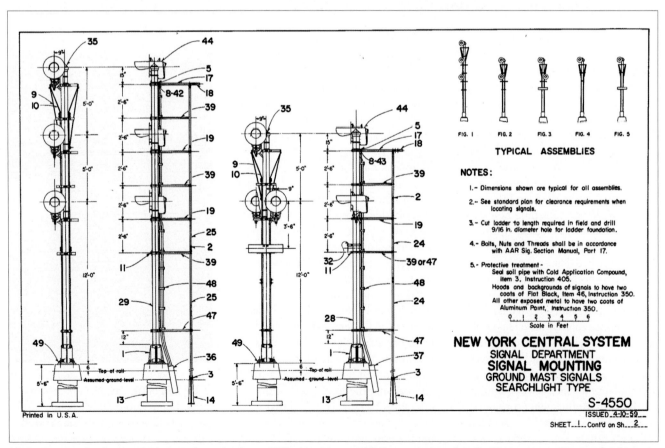

Note the standard mounting procedures in these GRS type SA searchlight mounting details. These were the standard head used at Frontier Yard in Buffalo, N.Y., and all points east.

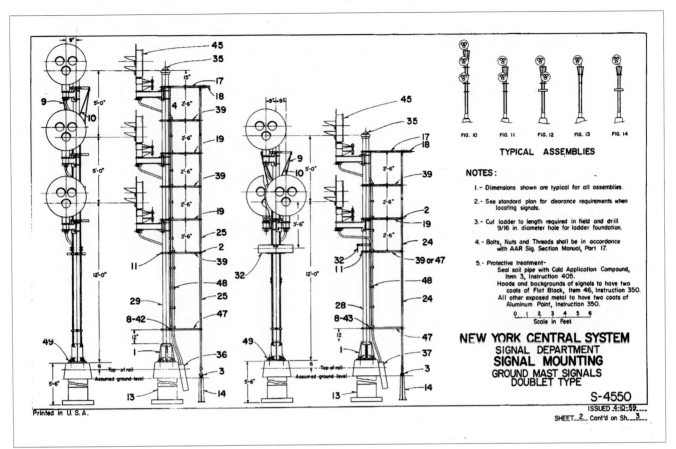

Within the diagram:

TYPICAL ASSEMBLIES

FIG. 10 FIG. 11 FIG. 12 FIG. 13 FIG. 14

NOTES:

1. - Dimensions shown are typical for all assemblies.

2. - See standard plan for clearance requirements when locating signals.

3. - Cut ladder to length required in field and drill 9/16 in. diameter hole for ladder foundation.

4. - Bolts, Nuts and Threads shall be in accordance with AAR Sig. Section Manual, Part 17.

5. - Protective treatment-
     Seal soil pipe with Cold Application Compound, Item 3, Instruction 405.
     Hoods and backgrounds of signals to have two coats of Flat Black, Item 46, Instruction 350.
     All other exposed metal to have two coats of Aluminum Paint, Instruction 350.

Scale in Feet

NEW YORK CENTRAL SYSTEM
SIGNAL DEPARTMENT
SIGNAL MOUNTING
GROUND MAST SIGNALS
DOUBLET TYPE

S-4550

ISSUED 4-12-59
SHEET 2 Cont'd on Sh. 3

Printed in U. S. A.

New York Central used several different types of signal heads in different parts of the system and hand standard plans for all. The GRS type G tri-light was the standard head used generally for all points west of Buffalo N.Y.

Much as the new interlocking installations improved safety and efficiency, however, each interlocking "plant" was essentially just an island of controlled switches and signals separated by miles of track that was either "dark"—no signals—or consisted of automatic signals only. Trains moved from one controlled island to another like ships on an ocean sailing from island to island.

At junctions and other interlocking plants, there was a vast improvement in control and flexibility versus train crews moving the switches themselves, but this was a far cry from a truly centralized and integrated system. Moreover, each interlocking had to be manned to operate its controlled switches and signals, and to coordinate via telegraph with other manned interlockings and the train dispatcher. Manual intervention was necessary for each and every train movement.

Once control of the interlockings began, it followed that trains could save time. Instead of slowing for

each interlocking prepared to stop, distant signals could be displayed to communicate the status of the interlocking ahead.

These "distant signals" were designed to be automatic, like the block signals along the main line, but these automatic signals changed depending on the aspect of the home signal as opposed to being separately controlled, 24. The concept of the distant signal also opened the door to great coordination between these independent interlocked locations, including the electrical remote control of adjacent interlockings and more distant locations.

Improving capacity

Inventors were hard at work developing improved signals technology and combinations. The Overlap system was developed for automatic block signals on a single-track main line. This eliminated the risk should two opposing trains (two trains moving toward each other) attempt to enter

a single track section in opposite directions simultaneously.

The Overlap system enabled the two trains to receive approach and stop indications on the single-track system alerting each of the other. Most early automatic block signal systems were wired on the Overlap principal—the Union Pacific and Southern Pacific, notably, on their long stretches of single-track territory across the largely empty western U.S.

In the early 1900s, the Absolute Permissive Block (APB) method of wiring signals on single-track main lines was developed. It provided a substantial capacity improvement on the Overlap system. The "Absolute" refers to this system being stop-and-stay for opposing train movements, and the "Permissive" for being stop-and-proceed for following train movements, 25. Almost all single-track signal systems built after 1920 followed APB principles, and APB principles continue in use to this day, whereas the remaining Overlap systems have largely

38

This overview of CP 282 looks west toward Syracuse on the Onondaga Cutoff. Note the powered turnouts and bungalow.

been replaced with APB systems.

Electric motors were improving, and began to be used in experiments to move the points on switches. The technology of lenses and light continued to develop as well. In 1911, Dr. William Churchill at Corning Glass's research facility in Corning, New York, was granted a patent for the "Doublet-Lens" combination for long range visibility of color-light signals, **26**.

Several years later, in 1916, Churchill, in combination with Arthur Holley Rudd of the Pennsylvania Railroad, was granted a patent for the final lamp configuration. This used a tungsten lamp arranged with reflectors to focus the beam and prevent outside light from entering and making the signal appear illuminated when it is not.

Combined with new signal yellow and lunar white glass lenses, this invention allowed signal light to be visible up to about 2,500 feet in broad daylight and greatly added to the safety of the system even in fog or adverse weather, **27**.

Starting in 1915 on the PRR Main Line between Overbrook and Paoli outside Philadelphia, Rudd began installation of an invention of his own, the now-famous Position-Light Signal. While versions of the position light in

Britain had predated Rudd's invention, the "PRR Position Light" came to be an iconic symbol of this railroad.

Consisting of large round black-painted heads with the new signal yellow lights arranged in straight-line rows vertically, horizontally, and on a diagonal, the new position lights dramatically increased signal visibility, simplified maintenance, worked reasonably well even in adverse weather conditions and were to some extent fault tolerant in that signal aspects were readable even if one of the lamps burned out.

Position light systems essentially replicated the positional information of a semaphore, but with lights, by using rows of the lights to indicate clear, two or three vertical lights; caution, two or three lights angled at 45 degrees to the vertical; and stop, two or three horizontal lights.

While color lights remained dominant across the nation, position lights had several advantages: several lights for each aspect had inherent redundancy, visibility was maximized since all of the lights were white, and any issue of a train crewman's color blindness was eliminated, **28**. In all cases signal visibility was increasing, and as visibility increased, so did the

effectiveness of the system.

What all this meant to superintendents and railroad management is that trains could travel with less distance between each movement, increasing capacity on each line. However, while electric signals could provide fail-safe protection, they could not by themselves convey authority to proceed. That authority would still have to come from the timetable or a manual train order. That led to the next big step forward: Centralized Traffic Control, or CTC.

Centralized Traffic Control

This next major leap in signal technology combined the visibility and safety of the electric color-light signal into an integrated, automated system that eliminated towers, operators, and TT&TO operation.

This pioneering signal advancement was made during the Roaring 20s by a small signal manufacturing and installation company called General Railway Signal Inc., or GRS for short. First on the New York Central in Ohio, and then on the Denver & Rio Grande Western Railroad (D&RGW) on its Royal Gorge Route main line over Tennessee Pass in Colorado, GRS developed a system where trains could run via signal indication authority alone, using remote-controlled signals and power-operated switches, **29**.

Instead of a complicated and unwieldy system of train class and priority, and train orders and timetables, the dispatcher now had sole authority and discretion to determine the priority and route of trains, and the ability to exercise that power in real time. Routes and priorities were delivered to trains by signal, and switches were lined by the dispatcher. Capacity of main lines often more than doubled, and armies of train-order operators were made redundant, **30**.

Centralized Traffic Control rapidly spread onto single-track railroads where traffic levels were high enough that double-tracking had previously seemed the only viable option, and then onto double-track railroads where traffic levels threatened expensive triple-tracking. Centralized Traffic Control then began to replace multiple main tracks: Four tracks operated with towers could become two. Two tracks with directional running could become one, **31**.

Two signaling firms quickly became the leaders in signal and interlocking construction and design for American railroads: Union Switch & Signal (US&S), founded by George Westinghouse and headquartered in Pittsburgh, Pa., and General Railway Signal (GRS), headquartered in Rochester, N.Y., **32**. Most railroads adopted the technology and standards

Norfolk Southern C40-9W no. 9434 storms out of Musconetcong Tunnel with train 212 in Pattenburg, N.J., in April 2013. This unique interlocking was created by NS during the split of Conrail in 1999. Part of Conrail's former Lehigh Valley main line, this tunnel was single-tracked to accommodate extra-height cars like the auto racks and stack cars in today's consist. The resulting interlocking, CP 64, includes the switches and home signals on both sides of the tunnel—creating an interlocking nearly 5,000 feet long.

Rio Grande GP30s No. 3007 and 3003 pull train No. 753 through the CTC positive (absolute) signals at Geneva, Utah on Oct. 21, 1987. An early pioneer in CTC, Rio Grande used distinctive "P" plates to mark its home signals standing for "Positive" and included a number plate on all signals systemwide. *James Belmont*

CTC over Rio Grande's Tennessee Pass, 1928

The principal contribution of signaling to railroads in the 20th century was its ability to deliver capacity and fluidity of train operations at a much lower cost than construction of additional main tracks. This was proven in 1928 with the installation of a pioneering Centralized Traffic Control (CTC) system on the highest standard-gauge mainline crossing of a mountain pass in North America—Denver & Rio Grande Western's Royal Gorge Route across Tennessee Pass in Colorado, at an altitude of 10,212 feet. The Royal Gorge Route main line was created in 1890 as a standard-gauge main line with transcontinental aspirations. It superseded an assortment of narrow-gauge branch lines built willy-nilly beginning in 1872 to profit on the traffic of mining bonanzas at Leadville, Red Cliff, and Aspen.

Most of this so-called transcontinental railroad was simply the widened-out narrow-gauge. The curvature and the grade profile were atrocious, the embankment was narrow and prone to catastrophic failure beneath trains when saturated by snowmelt or rainfall, the track itself used light rail and untreated, unplated ties, and there was no signaling whatsoever.

In the 1920s, the Rio Grande came into the control of the Missouri Pacific. The MoPac had ambitions of using itself, the Rio Grande, and the Western Pacific to create a viable competitor to the Union Pacific/Southern Pacific Overland Route, the Santa Fe, and the Southern Pacific Sunset Route, for traffic between the Mississippi River gateways and the West Coast. It was willing to spend millions to accomplish this goal. And in this era, this decision looked rational. Trucking was scarcely an invention and thought to be a meaningful transportation tool for only local and itinerant movements of light goods and farmstuffs.

The Interstate Commerce Commission had prescribed minimum rates to prohibit the strongest railroads with the best routes from seizing all the traffic of smaller railroads with more costly routes and thereby starving thousands of communities across the

U.S. served by smaller railroads of viable transportation equitable in cost with more fortunately located communities served by large railroads.

Thus, beginning in 1925, the MoPac began to reconstruct the Rio Grande. The Royal Gorge Route between Pueblo and Salt Lake City was massively realigned to reduce sharp curves, undulating grades, and short, steep stretches that limited train tonnage. Timber bridges were replaced with steel. Light rail and unplated, untreated ties were replaced with pressure-treated ties, each with substantial tie plates to spread the weight of the rail and provide better spiking to resist gauge-widening on curves. Slag and sized gravel ballast replaced the native clays and dirt of the embankment and ditches. Signaling—for the first time!—was installed on the Rio Grande; unlike its western peers that had signaled their principal main lines starting in the 1890s, the Rio Grande in 1925 was innocent of automatic block signals.

Tennessee Pass presented a particular problem. The summit of the Continental Divide, it featured a 3 percent helper grade eastward from Minturn to Tennessee Pass, 20.5 miles, gaining 2,400 feet of elevation. Most of the west side of the pass had been double-tracked, but a section of 5.5 miles of single-track—almost all of it 3 percent—remained. This single-track section was book-ended by the 2,550-foot long Tennessee Pass Tunnel at the east end, and the 242-foot long Pando Tunnel at the west, and much of it was chiseled into a mountainside. By 1925 there were four to six passenger trains and three to 10 freight trains each way daily, plus five to 16 light helpers daily returning to Minturn after helping trains to the pass. Thus on a busy day, 48 train movements struggled for a slot on the single-track section.

General Railway Signal had the right solution at the right time. Instead of expensive excavation for a second main track and parallel tunnels to the Tennessee Pass and Pando tunnels, GRS thought its new Centralized Traffic Control system could provide nearly the capacity of double track,

at a fraction of the cost. Thus in 1928, the second-ever CTC system was installed, between the east switch of the Tennessee Pass siding and the beginning of double-track at Deen, just west of the Pando Tunnel.

Even though CTC was much cheaper than a second main track, it was still expensive. Rather than install power switches at every location, Rio Grande installed them only at the east end of Tennessee Pass. Spring switches were installed at the beginning of double-track at Deen, and on each end of Mitchell, a 2.2 mile long siding just west of the Tennessee Pass Tunnel that became an effective short stretch of double-track. Hand-throw switches remained at the west end of the Tennessee Pass siding, where the CTC control operator could see them from his office in the Tennessee Pass depot, and at a universal crossover in the middle of the double-track section at Mitchell. The control operator used codes transmitted from a siren at the west end of Tennessee Pass siding to instruct train crews when to operate switches, and which switches to operate. Eastbound trains signaled their arrival into CTC territory at Deen to the control operator at Tennessee Pass by means of whistle signals that were relayed by an annunciator system to a speaker in the operator's office.

At West Tennessee Pass, while the interlocking used hand-throw switches, authority to enter the interlocking was by signal indication. These didn't need to be power switches; there was small value to powering up these turnouts as all trains were required to stop at Tennessee Pass anyway, for inspection of the train and brakes. Moreover, westbound freight trains had to turn up retainers before stepping onto the 3 percent descent, and eastbound trains had to cut out helpers.

Accordingly, Tennessee Pass was a Yard Limits station—during the steam era, almost every station along the Rio Grande with anything other than just a siding was classified as a Yard Limits station for just this reason. Westward trains arriving at Tennessee Pass had their routes directed by signal

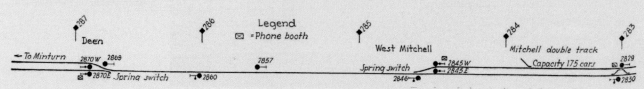

indication at East Tennessee Pass to use the main track or one of the two 100-car passing sidings. The No. 2 siding to the south side of the main track was the normal westward route. The No. 1 siding on the north side of the main track was the normal eastward route, as the wye on which helpers turned, and a helper pocket track, sprung from the No. 1 siding. The main track was suitable for train movements in either direction. Crossovers just beyond each leg of the wye connected the No. 1 siding and the main track, enabling an eastward train arriving on the main track to cut out its swing helper and for the helper escape through the No. 1 siding to the wye or the pocket track.

There were more idiosyncrasies stemming from the newness and novelty of CTC. In 1928, today's system of informing train crews of the difference between a CTC signal that granted authority for train movement and an ordinary automatic block signal that only advised of track conditions ahead had yet to be worked out. Rio Grande and GRS instead applied a "marker" signal to each automatic block signal. The marker signal consisted of a small head beneath the main three-color head that lit red to identify the signal as a Stop and Stay. The signal lens was masked so that a red "P" showed, this indicated "Positive" and meant Stop and Stay. (Most railroads called a Stop and Stay signal an "Absolute;" Rio Grande used "Positive," which meant the same thing, for most of its history. Later, the P marker lights were replaced with a letter P on a triangular nameplate affixed to the signal, the P commonly using clear or red glass beads to provide reflectivity when illuminated by a locomotive headlight.)

Mitchell normally operated directionally, with westward trains on Main No. 1 (the northernmost track) and eastward trains on Main No. 2 (the southernmost track). "Wrong way" movements could be made on either track if the train crew hand-operated the spring switch. If the control operator at Tennessee Pass wanted an eastward train to take Main No. 1 in preference to the usual Main No. 2, he didn't simply give it a Proceed indication under this early system.

Instead, the signal would display "stop" causing the head-end brakeman to walk to the phone booth at the crossovers, call the control operator, and receive permission to hand-operate the switch. The control operator would then request a Proceed indication on his console. The CTC machine was able to determine when the switch was lined and locked for Main No. 1. If it detected no conflicting moves, it would provide either a Proceed or Approach indication to the eastward signal at West Mitchell, the "wrong main."

Mitchell also had a universal crossover with directional ABS signals on the eastward and westward mains at this location informing train crew that the turnouts were either normal or reversed, and the train ahead was clear or occupied. The control operator would provide instructions to operate this crossover, as needed, to a train at either West Mitchell or West Tennessee Pass. Capacity of Mitchell was 103 cars east of the crossovers and 175 cars west of the crossovers. The crossovers were a nice way to "hide" light helpers from through trains, yet get them out of Tennessee Pass's sidings expeditiously to make room for trains cutting out helpers or setting up retainers at Tennessee Pass.

In railroad signal engineering, color-light signal terminology and symbology is identical to semaphore terminology, thus "position" is used to describe the number of lights just as it would describe the number of positions a semaphore arm could take. The upper three-position heads provided, from top to bottom, a green aspect indicating proceed, a yellow aspect indicating proceed, but approach the next signal ready to stop, and a red aspect indicating stop. All signal heads except the westward signal at East Tennessee Pass were single heads with three lights; the westward signal at East Tennessee Pass was the only two-head signal in the installation. Its lower, two-position head provided lunar (white) and red aspects to indicate route. Thus a G/R or Y/R aspect indicated proceed on main track; a R/L indicated take siding, and a R/R aspect indicated stop.

All positive signals were equipped with the additional marker signal to indicate these were Stop and Stay signals. A single pair of intermediates between West Mitchell and Deen—which were offset due to sight lines on curves—did not have the marker lights as these were Stop, Then Proceed signals. Because the CTC at Tennessee Pass was really an overlay on the APB-ABS system the D&RGW was concurrently installing between Pueblo, Colorado, and Salt Lake City, Utah, it would follow that the CTC block signals at Tennessee Pass would have the same aspects and indications as the APB-ABS block signals.

It's worth noting that Rio Grande had a second "proto-CTC" system as well, installed the following year on its other busy mountain helper grade, Soldier Summit in Utah, 25 miles of double-track between Helper and Colton, which had a 2.4 percent helper grade westward. This was termed a "reverse-signaled APB-ABS system" by both GRS and Rio Grande, rather than CTC, as several operators were employed both to control signals and turnouts at several locations where trains could cross over between main tracks or take center sidings to permit overtakes. This again was not a full CTC system due to cost, as well as because the technology to "fully CTC" such a complex and lengthy territory had yet to be developed.

GRS's CTC system at Tennessee Pass solved Rio Grande's capacity problem. Double-tracking was never required even with the crush of World War II traffic. After the war, traffic over Tennessee Pass declined steeply as Rio Grande favored the shorter, faster Moffat Tunnel Route via Denver, and because Denver's population and industry grew rapidly while Pueblo's did not grow at all. In 1958, the second main track between Minturn and Deen was removed, and new CTC was installed over Tennessee Pass, replacing this pioneering system. Today even this CTC is silent, with the shift of through traffic from the former Rio Grande through Colorado to the Union Pacific through Wyoming.—*Mark W. Hemphill*

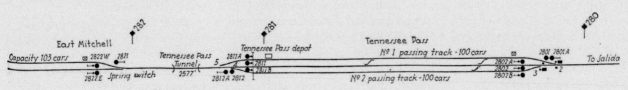

Clear winter skies highlight the eastward home signals at CP 335 on the former NYC Water Level Route, now CSX's Chicago Line. GRS searchlights, installed atop signal bridges over four main tracks in the 1940s, will soon be replaced by LED color-light signals on ground masts. Coincidentally, these new signals were cut-in during 2013 and 2014 as the author cut in models of the GRS signals they replaced! *Nick Anshant*

of one or the other makers. Union Switch & Signal supplied the famous now-patented Pennsylvania Railroad position light signals and the color-light signals for Norfolk Western and Chesapeake & Ohio, **33**, and was the preferred supplier for the "Harriman roads"—Union Pacific and Southern Pacific.

General Railway Signal was the favored company of the New York Central; the "Hill Roads"—the Chicago, Burlington & Quincy; Great Northern; Northern Pacific; and Spokane, Portland & Seattle; and the "Gould Roads"—the Rio Grande; Western Pacific; Missouri Pacific.

But there was considerable overlap. Union Pacific, for example, gave most of its automatic block signal business to US&S, but its interlockings were often manufactured by GRS. General Railway Signal moved to perfect the electric motor to move switch points. Competitors Federal Signal Company followed suit until being purchased by GRS in 1923.

Union Switch & Signal pioneered the electro-pneumatic power

interlocking, using air pressure to move switch points, and also developed an electric motor for switch points. Competitor manufacturers joined the growing market as well, including companies like Western Railroad Supply Company, **34**.

The eventual domination of the market by US&S and GRS fostered greater commonality of parts and systems. Today, both are owned by parent automation companies and remain competitors. Modern railroads often use both suppliers, since in many cases routes are now combined through mergers over several predecessor railroads, who may have used one or the other.

Two dominant styles of signal rules developed: "Speed Signaling," where the aspect conveys an allowable speed limit only, regardless of whatever route the dispatcher might have selected, and "Route Signaling," where the aspect conveyed a particular route lined through the plant and the employee is responsible for knowing and adhering to the correct speed limit through each turnout and on each track, which are

published in the employee timetable, **35**.

Typically, railroads in the Northeast, with highly complex routes and interlockings, used Speed Signaling, while railroads in the West with vast stretches of single main track with scattered sidings, used Route Signaling, with some mixing of systems in the Midwest and South.

While part of this divergence originated with institutions, locations and personalities, a significant factor influencing design was that traffic in the congested, high traffic and high-density East Coast to Chicago routes demanded more complicated interlockings so that having a different aspect displayed for each route in complicated interlockings was cumbersome, if not impossible, **36**. Therefore, Speed Signaling conveyed a speed through the aligned route instead of describing exactly which route was aligned.

As designs evolved, the original purely mechanical interlocking system was improved by adding powered controls and components. Each railroad tended to put its own stamp

41

New ground-mast signals stand as agents of change with a backdrop of classic GRS searchlights on an NYC signal bridge at MP 298, in Warners, N.Y. On important main lines, railroads cannot tolerate the delay and congestion of operations without signals, so any change must be made as quickly as possible to get trains running again. Cutover day is still more than a year off; so the ground masts once tested will be turned aside and bagged so as not to confuse crews until the day of the cutover arrives. *Nick Anshant*

on the signals for its lines, and often signals or their details were unique to the point they could be used to tell what company owned the railroad, **37**. Improved electrical motors were incorporated into the design and electrical relay-based interlocking became more common, **38**. Switch points were moved by electrical motors or on some roads by pneumatic systems and compressed air.

Today, almost all new interlockings are built around field hardware operating via solid-state electronics and vital computer logic, **39**. Fortunately for those modeling more modern railroads, solid-state prototypes allow (relatively) easy means to re-create the look and feel of the prototype dispatcher screen.

Positive Train Control

The latest development in railroad signaling, and one that is changing the face of modern rights-of-way across the United States, is Positive Train Control, known in the industry as PTC.

After a series of fatal accidents attributed to human error in the cab

(i.e., the engineer) through the 1990s and 2000s, political pressure increased on the government to require a safer way of controlling trains to eliminate engineer error. Congress mandated a system be developed and implemented by the industry by 2015 for all main track that carries a minimum of 5 million gross tons per year, as well as on most, but not all, lines where passenger trains operate. Further, if a line passes a certain threshold of hazardous material tonnage, PTC is also required, **40**.

Depending on the system selected, PTC uses a combination of GPS coordinates or locally installed transponders, satellite and cellular communications, and onboard safety and braking systems to bring a train to a stop before colliding with another train, passing a stop signal, or entering a work zone, or traveling at excessive speed.

Due to the massive cost and challenge of the installation, particularly in the complicated trackwork of urban junctions, the

deadline in many cases moved to January 2021. Because relay-based signaling is not readily compatible with PTC, railroads upgraded most of their remaining legacy systems to microprocessor control systems, and replaced old incandescent-bulb signaling with LED color-light signaling, **41**.

While PTC can function as a standalone system for train control, that is not the prevalent installation in the United States. Instead, PTC has usually been installed as a safety overlay to a CTC system. As a result, the signal aspects of most railroads and routes have not been altered due to the installation of PTC. From our perspective as modelers, most aspects look the same now as they did before PTC was mandated.

Positive Train Control is the latest change to the world of signaling but will not be the last. History continues to be made by railroads and their signal systems and our next step is to understand how this relates to our model railroads.

CHAPTER TWO

Signal system basics: knowing your options

Conrail train COSE comes out from beneath the aspects and interlocking limits at CP 277 on the Onondaga Cutoff. Light-emitting diode signals are visible from a wider angle than the prototype so as to allow operators to see them from the aisle.

In addition to the systems covered in the first chapter of this book, early signaling systems included train-order signals and manual-block signals. Both systems existed largely before radio use was common. Both train-order and manual-block signals operated by hand: the signals are manually positioned to convey certain messages to train crews.

Maumee Route local freight No. 20 prepares to work at Delphia. The manual signal here is clear for the diamond, with the blade in a vertical position for the Maumee. The train-order signal at the station operator's office also shows clear in both directions. *Bill Darnaby*

Dwarf signals are used in a variety of situations with limited clearances and interlockings. The westbound signals governing movement into busy CP 285 in East Syracuse, N.Y., show a medium-clear aspect for a train leaving Dewitt Yard.

In those systems there is no electrical or mechanical verification whether a train is occupying a certain track. Train order signals were used for many years to communicate to an approaching train whether new written orders had been addressed to the train. If the train-order signal was set horizontally, that meant the operator had received a message from the dispatcher and that the train needed to slow or stop to allow that train to receive the written order, **1**.

Manual-block signals, on the other hand, were a different system used to convey to approaching trains the message that the next block ahead was clear or occupied after the operator verified that with the next operator up the line. These methods worked well but required labor-intensive manual intervention.

As they were dependent on effective verbal and written communication carried out by humans, without mechanical or electrical fail-safe systems, they also carried the constant danger of a mistake—and a mistake with train movements is rarely a small mistake.

Saxby's patents and inventions, and those inventions that followed throughout railroading, mostly worked to automate signals, or to provide an automatic safety check at turnout locations. Automatic signals operating without human intervention communicated information to train crews about their ability to safely proceed: when, where, and how, by indicating speed, route, whether to stop or proceed, and the integrity of the track ahead, i.e., broken rails. In model form, these signals can be built to provide those same communications except, of course, for broken rails.

You've heard it before: model railroading is full of compromise and adaptation. Across all scales, despite what prototype is followed and regardless of era, every layout and model involves many compromises and adaptations. It follows that

Another loaded coal train enters the interlocking at Sandstone, W.Va., on the former Chesapeake & Ohio main line. The signal bridge supports the home signals for eastbounds and marks the western limit of the interlocking.

model railroad signals involve some compromise and adaptation too, but in many respects signaling basics on a model railroad closely follow the prototype practice. Simply put, it is difficult to achieve realistic model signals without understanding prototype signaling, how it works, why location matters, and how it affects train movements, **2**.

Whether you are reading this book to install a simple block signal, create interlockings, or just to learn, the basics are the same.

Track circuits— detected sections

Signal systems detect trains through the means of the train (or locomotive, or single rail car) interrupting an electrical circuit that runs through the rails, **3**. The genius of the prototype signal system is that it uses the rail, track, and the steel or wrought-iron wheelset/ axle assemblies in the locomotives and cars themselves to accomplish this. The railroad term for this is a "track circuit." It works as follows, **4**.

- The track on which signaling is desired is divided into track circuits, which are wired so as to create detected sections using insulated

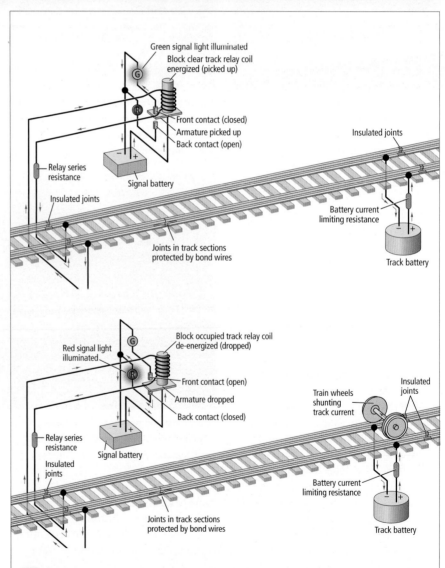

4 These are the components of a prototype signal system, showing how the circuit works when it's open (top) and closed (bottom) by the wheels and axles of locomotives and rolling stock.

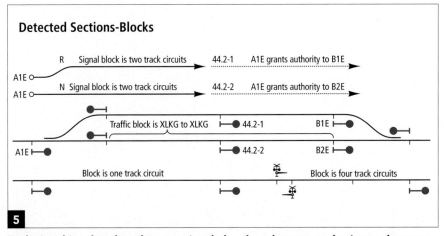

Detected Sections-Blocks

R   Signal block is two track circuits   44.2-1   A1E grants authority to B1E

A1E

N   Signal block is two track circuits   44.2-2   A1E grants authority to B2E

A1E

Traffic block is XLKG to XLKG   44.2-1   B1E

A1E   44.2-2   B2E

Block is one track circuit   Block is four track circuits

5

Each signal is related to the next signal ahead, and grants authority to that next signal. Several track circuits can be part of any detected section.

6

The semaphores indicate stop as a train passes through a block on Steve Barkley's HO scale Northern Pacific layout. Steve uses computer software to control his signals. *Bob Werre*

joints applied to each rail. The insulated joints are opposite of each other. Each block or detected section is comprised of one or more track circuits.

- The length of a detected section corresponds to the desired spacing of signals. Signal spacing is determined by the maximum braking distances of the trains that will be operated on the track and the maximum speed at which these trains operate. Obviously, it wouldn't do to have a signal indicating "Proceed" spaced so closely to a signal indicating "Stop" if the train couldn't brake to a stop before it passed the Stop signal. Freight trains usually have longer braking distances than passenger trains.

- A low-voltage power supply, usually a DC battery, is connected to one end of the track circuit. The two poles of the battery are connected to opposite rails.

- At the other end of the track circuit, which is typically several thousand feet away from the battery, a wire is connected from each rail to a relay. This completes the electrical circuit.

- Current flowing through the circuit energizes the relay, which closes electrical contacts that complete a separate electrical circuit that powers the signal itself. If there is no train or railcar occupying this detected section, the signal is energized and the signal by means of color light,

color position, or mechanical arm indicates that the track section is clear of trains, providing a "Proceed" indication.

- When a train, locomotive, or rail car enters the detected section, electrical current now has a shorter path of lower resistance between the two poles of the battery than through the relay. The relay is de-energized

7

Santa Fe 808 leads an eastbound out of the yard at Clovis and meets a westbound headed up by an F45 and some Conrail run-through power. The yard is under local control but is under CTC rules past this point. The signal is by Tomar.

Sammy Carlile

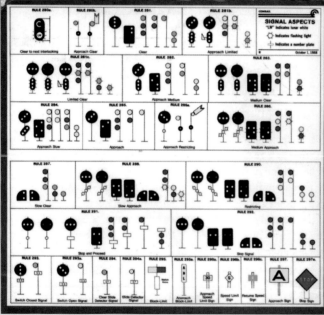

Signal aspect charts

The need for capacity and early success of signaling drove railroads to pursue it with zeal throughout the late 1800s and early 1900s. As aspects became more complicated than simple red, yellow, or green, crews needed an easy way to learn the aspects and what their indications meant. Most railroads developed "signal aspect charts" that could be printed on cards or in the employee timetable, and became part of the physical characteristics that crews were required to commit to memory in order to be considered qualified to operate trains over that territory. Aspects differed from railroad to railroad. Developing an aspect chart for your railroad is a fun way to learn more about signaling, and helps your operators in the same way as the prototype. Aspects added second and third heads and in some cases auxiliary lights to provide for different indications and to dictate different speed limits or routes.

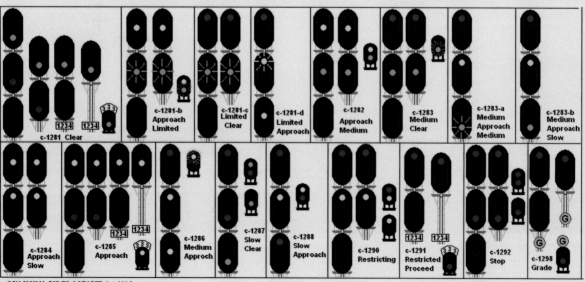

281	A281ᵃ	282	282A	283	285	A285ᵇ	286	287	288	290	291	292
CLEAR	CLEAR	APPROACH MEDIUM	ADVANCED APPROACH	MEDIUM CLEAR	APPROACH	CAUTION SIGNAL	MEDIUM APPROACH	SLOW CLEAR	SLOW APPROACH	RESTRICTING	STOP AND PROCEED	STOP

a. Used only in nonautomatic block territory.

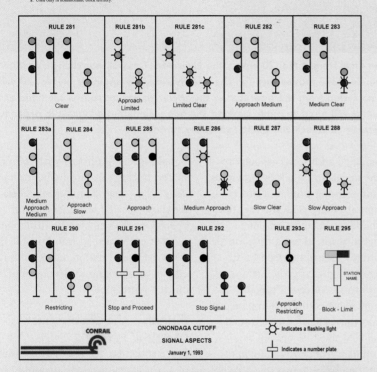

Signal aspect diagrams:

RULE 281 — Clear	RULE 281b — Approach Limited	RULE 281c — Limited Clear	RULE 282 — Approach Medium	RULE 283 — Medium Clear
RULE 283a — Medium Approach Medium	RULE 284 — Approach Slow	RULE 285 — Approach	RULE 286 — Medium Approach	RULE 287 — Slow Clear	RULE 288 — Slow Approach
RULE 290 — Restricting	RULE 291 — Stop and Proceed	RULE 292 — Stop Signal	RULE 293c — Approach Restricting	RULE 295 — Block - Limit

CONRAIL — ONONDAGA CUTOFF — SIGNAL ASPECTS — January 1, 1993

Indicates a flashing light
Indicates a number plate

CONRAIL

RULE 281
NAME: Clear
INDICATION: Proceed not exceeding Normal Speed.

RULE 281b
NAME: Approach Limited
INDICATION: Proceed approaching next signal at Limited Speed.

RULE 281c
NAME: Limited Clear
INDICATION: Proceed; Limited Speed within interlocking limits.

RULE 282
NAME: Approach Medium
INDICATION: Proceed approaching next signal at Medium Speed.

RULE 283
NAME: Medium Clear
INDICATION: Proceed; Medium Speed within interlocking limits.

RULE 283a
NAME: Medium Approach Medium
INDICATION: Proceed at Medium Speed until entire train clears interlocking, then approach the next signal at Medium Speed.

RULE 284
NAME: Approach Slow
INDICATION: Proceed approaching the next signal at Slow Speed.

RULE 285
NAME: Approach
INDICATION: Proceed prepared to stop at next signal.

RULE 286
NAME: Medium Approach
INDICATION: Proceed at Medium Speed, prepared to stop at next signal.

RULE 287
NAME: Slow Clear
INDICATION: Proceed; Slow Speed within interlocking limits.

RULE 288
NAME: Slow Approach
INDICATION: Proceed prepared to stop at next signal; Slow Speed within interlocking limits; approach the next signal at Medium Speed.

RULE 290
NAME: Restricting
INDICATION: Proceed at Restricted Speed until entire train has passed a more favorable signal or entered MBS

RULE 291
NAME: Stop and Proceed
INDICATION: Stop; then proceed at Restricted Speed until entire train has passed a more favorable signal or entered MBS territory.

RULE 292
NAME: Stop Signal
INDICATION: Stop.

RULE 293c
NAME: Approach Restricting
INDICATION: Proceed prepared to stop at hand operated switches and at next signal.

RULE 295
NAME: Block - Limit
INDICATION: Limit of the Block.

SPEEDS

NORMAL SPEED: The maximum authorized speed.

LIMITED SPEED: For passenger trains, not exceeding 45 miles per hour; for freight trains, not exceeding 40 miles per hour.

MEDIUM SPEED: Not exceeding 30 miles per hour.

SLOW SPEED: Not exceeding 15 miles per hour.

RESTRICTED SPEED: Prepared to stop within one-half the range of vision, but not exceeding 20 mph outside interlocking limits, nor 15 mph within interlocking limits. Speed applies to entire movement.

and as it "drops out" it opens the electrical circuit that powers the signal. The signal now changes to a "Stop" indication to alert other trains that this section of track is occupied.

- The track circuit is designed on fail-safe principles. Any break in the track circuit de-energizes the relay and sets the signal to a "Stop" indication. This could be a power failure, a wire break, or a broken rail. Even the relays are mounted so that gravity must be overcome by electromagnetic force to lift the lower contacts up until they touch the upper contacts and close the relay; if power fails for any reason, the lower relay contacts obey gravity and fall away. Only a complete and functioning system provides a "Proceed" indication.

Multiple blocks, or detected sections, along a railroad line are connected to each other through relays so that the logic relies on information about the condition of the adjacent detected sections, **5**. For example, if one block detects the presence of a train, and sets the signals at either end of it at "Stop," the adjacent track circuits will set their signals at their far ends at "Approach."

Signals have both aspects and indications. The "aspect" is the color, position, or condition of a signal. For example, a signal may be colored red, green, yellow, blue, or "lunar" (white) or consist of three red or non-colored lights in a horizontal line, or the light may flash, or the signal may be a mechanical "semaphore" that can be moved into the vertical, horizontal, or diagonal position, or the signal may be a combination of lights and semaphores. All of these are called "aspects." The "indication" is the instruction to the train that is conveyed by the aspect. For example, a green signal aspect indicates "Proceed." A horizontal semaphore aspect indicates "Stop," **6**.

This linear progression is the basic for automatic block signal systems. While individual railroads often had differing ideas about the aspects of their signals and the information conveyed by each aspect, the logic is the same on all railroads, and in general the aspects are too. In basic terms—individual railroads vary in the words they use but the intent is the same—red lights, multiple lights of any color arranged in a horizontal line, or a horizontal semaphore blade mean "Stop," the block ahead is occupied or a route has not been cleared.

Yellow lights, multiple lights arranged in a diagonal line, or a diagonal semaphore blade means "Approach," that the next detected section ahead has a Stop indication at its far end, and speed must be reduced accordingly.

Green lights, multiple lights arranged in a vertical line, or a vertical semaphore blade means "Proceed," that the block ahead is clear, and the next block after that is either Proceed or Approach. And similarly, trains leave in their wake a signal progression of Stop, Approach, and Proceed, providing information to trains behind them.

On top of this basic system, most railroads developed numerous additional signal aspects and indications to provide information to trains about the maximum safe speed they could travel, the route they would take, and in some cases whether they could safely occupy a block even though there was another train within that block.

For example, many railroads added a "fourth aspect" to the basic three, consisting of a flashing yellow light,

Maumee local freight No. 20 works the New York Central interchange at Miami Junction. To make moves through the interlocking, the engineer on No. 20 will need permission from the operator at the tower to ensure routes are lined and locked, and will need to move beyond the home semaphore signals in order for the operator to unlock the plant and throw turnouts. *Bill Darnaby*

which enabled additional capacity to be added to existing track by providing additional warning time of a Stop indication ahead. (Recall the mention of safe braking distances earlier.)

Some railroads added a fifth aspect consisting of a flashing green light, allowing for higher speeds. Each different aspect conveys a specific indication. Each combination of aspect and indication is a rule in each road's rulebook that must be obeyed as a condition of continued employment. Each railroad had its own rulebook for

signal aspects. Railroads with joint or shared trackage in terminals or on joint lines often created unique rulebooks for those specific terminal or joint operations that melded the different rules of each railroad into one, for the train crews and maintenance-of-way employees working in that terminal or on that joint line.

Signals—the visible part of signal systems

Once you enter the realm of dreaming of a working signal system, and once

The interlocking at Fairmont, Ohio, on the Maumee is a crossing of the Baltimore & Ohio with the Maumee, with the B&O's distinctive color position lights guarding the diamonds. Note the train-order signal at left in front of the Maumee Station. *Bill Darnaby*

The three-head signal mast guards the entrance to CP 282 from the Morristown & Eastern on the Onondaga Cutoff. General Railway Signals Co. signal heads with the distinctive 18"-diameter backdrop rings, as opposed to the more typical 36" backdrop rings, tell us we are in former NYC territory.

Conrail ML-482 comes east at dusk through the interlocking at CP 280, passing Onondaga Yard on its trip across central New York.

Amtrak train No. 296 from Buffalo, N.Y., to New York City via the Onondaga Cutoff rushes toward its station stop at Fayetteville, N.Y., and a clear aspect on the 278 automatic signals.

some of the basics are understood, it is important to know what sort of commitment is required for different systems. Thanks to the wonders of modern manufacturing, signal modelers have a lot of choices and places to start. You may know what system your favorite prototype used at a certain spot, or you may not; you may be a freelance modeler looking for a working system, or perhaps you would like to model a certain prototype location, including all the options and custom details available in a system.

Like with other areas of model railroading, you will need to consider quality, scale fidelity, availability, and cost in deciding what signals to use. The benefit to off-the-shelf units is they are relatively common at model stores and online, and some are backed with a warranty. They are usually

available assembled, wired, and lit, and some even come with plugs installed for an easy plug-in system, **7**.

Limitations to those systems are that many are "one-size-fits-all" and don't include options for customized heads or auxiliary lamps or bases, and they may not be close enough to scale to satisfy you.

An important step in selecting signals, as with your other models, is era. Like rolling stock, signals have changed over time on different routes, and you will want to look at prototype photos to see what was working in your era on your modeled lines.

But fortunately, signals are much more long-lived than rolling stock or locomotives, and the large iron and steel hardware components of most signal systems (heads, masts, cases, and instrument houses) installed on

U.S. railroads lasted for at least a half-century before being retired in favor of improved and updated equipment.

Most major mainline railroads in the United States first installed semaphore signals between 1900 and 1920, **8**, which in many cases lasted until the 1960s when they were replaced with color-light signals. Railroads that first installed color-light signals in the 1920s often did not replace them until after 2010, in conjunction with implementation of Positive Train Control. Some semaphores lasted more than a century. Some color-lights are now more than a century old as well.

Note that the internal electrical equipment has often been revised, often more than once, but the external hardware, which is what we model, still looks the same, **9**. Signal aspects

A grungy GP35 is on the point of a road switcher at Joel, Tex. The engineer sees the approach signal and he has reduced his speed since the train will be stopping on the main to work an industry and the dispatcher has only cleared the train to the next signal. A pushbutton on the fascia can be unlocked by the dispatcher during operation sessions so the crews can use the turnout in hand-throw mode. Small details such as signal buildings, signal maintainers' truck, propane tanks, and switch motors help to set the scene. The signals are by BLMA. *Sammy Carlile*

are often changed too, even though the large iron hardware stays the same, so the key here, if prototypical accuracy is important, is to obtain a copy of the correct rule book for the railroad you wish to model, for the era you want to model.

Integrated Signal Systems (ISS) based in Florida and Atlas Model Railroad Company based in New Jersey both offer components and signals to model automated systems. Both ISS and Atlas offer boards that control signals. Atlas offers several styles of signal head and masts and offers still others through its former "BLMA" line of products. These boards come with instructions and "plug & play" offerings that can allow you to quickly develop a working system. Other manufacturers of signals include NJ International, Oregon Railway Supply, Bachmann, Walthers, Details West, and others. Different companies provide different models from which each modeler can review and select.

Another option for signals is to have them custom-built, **10**. Before you shy away from this option, there are several angles to consider. First, almost all prototype systems include significant customization. Second, while common signal types are available in most scales off the shelf, few of the more complicated ones are. Third, there are several sources for customized signals and most will work with you to ensure you get what you are looking for. Finally, and critically, you've taken on

The New York Central crossings at Edison on Bill Darnaby's Maumee Route includes a simulated armstrong interlocking plant, with the lock, switch, and signal levers located on the fascia in front of the tower. *Bill Darnaby*

signaling on your layout as a significant part of your hobby.

From experience, I can tell you that working signals will become a major focal point and one of the first things people notice. Given the attention they receive, signals are worth your investment—much like your favorite locomotive would be, except signals are there for all your engines to pass by, **11**. Signals are always visible to every passing train and to visitors. Given your preferred price point, consider buying signals over time and spreading out the cost to ensure you get what you will enjoy looking at for years to come.

An early pioneer in model railroad signaling is Bruce Chubb, whose layout and control systems are legendary in

model railroad operation. Bruce is the owner of the Computer Model Railroad Interface (C/MRI), and a website (jlcenterprises.net) that offers many components and parts to make a system work, including detection and turnout/signal control. Bruce owns JLC Enterprises, which sells all the components with excellent documentation for installation and use. There is extensive documentation of C/MRI online and the system was the feature of multiple-part series in *Model Railroader* magazine several times in the 1980s and 1990s.

What are your expectations for your railroad, **12**? This is a decision we are examining early so as to allow for you to have some guidance in the

Photo Electric custom-built this Union Switch & Signal CTC machine for Tony Koester's Allegheny Midland. Control Train Components, CTCParts.com, now markets these components. The wiring was planned around Bruce Chubb's Computer/Model Railroad Interface software and detectors. Much of the hardware was from salvaged US&S machines. *Tony Koester*

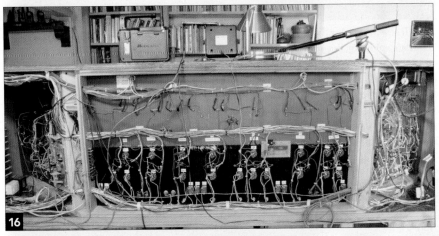

Several notable model railroads around the country use repurposed railroad CTC panels or replicas constructed in a similar manner for layout control. On Phil Monat's Delaware & Susquehanna, Phil created a CTC machine using C/MRI components and parts from a variety of sources. While beyond the scope of this book, these projects are a wonderful tribute to the original CTC machines in their heyday. *Phil Monat*

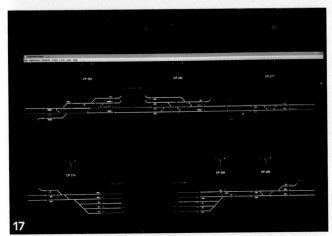

This is the CATS dispatcher panel for my Onondaga Cutoff. Train NPSE is shown crossing over from track 2 to track 1 at CP 282 and has a route all the way to CP 274. WAON-10, a local way freight, approaches CP 277 on track 2 and will enter Onondaga Yard at CP 280 once NPSE clears.

Here's the interior of ALTO tower in Altoona, Pa., near the stroke of midnight on an oddly warm February night in 2011. The original US&S interlocking machine for ALTO is to the left with its model board lit above. Jeannie Fouse, tonight's operator, is at her desk with the lineup on the screen to her right, standard clock, radio and phone in front of her, and the CTC machine from right to left for CP ANTIS, CP ROSE, and CP WORKS, all interlockings east of ALTO. A separate, smaller CTC machine at extreme left controls CP SLOPE to the west. *J. Alex Lang*

early steps. Each of the methods of providing signaling for your railroad has some merit and may be the path you select, **13**. Some railroads only need an automatic system, which is available in different forms off the shelf. Other railroads will use combinations of automatic and controlled systems, with some add-on features that have recently become available included in modern signal hardware. The most complicated systems will include computer- or machine-controlled signals at interlockings, with or without automatic intermediate signals, all wired to work from a certain location on site or via software on a network or the internet.

For those who are looking to build a system that allows dispatcher or operator control of working signals, there are three primary methods of control. Each is based on a prototype and each has merit depending on your specific desires or the practices of your prototype.

First, we can control your railroad

Jack Trabachino stands as a leverman ready to accept direction from Jerry Dziedzic, playing the role of operator, seated at the desk at Harris Tower in Harrisburg, Pa., a former Pennsylvania RR interlocking on the railroad's main line. The Union Switch & Signal machine and tower have been restored by the Harrisburg Chapter of the National Railroad Historical Society. The chapter runs a simulated "operating session" on a regular basis using the historic tower and massive interlocking machine, with the interlocking mechanism restored and now linked to JMRI on a PC, and wired to accept input from a lineup in JMRI that simulates an actual railroad operating experience.

New York, Susquehanna & Western No. 101, a mail and express train whose consist includes an extra coach seating a railfan group, glides through the crossover at Sparta Junction on Jerry Dziedzic's HO scale layout while one of Lehigh & Hudson River's USRA light Mikados waits. Light-emitting diode technology has greatly improved model railroad signals.

21 Two levers are required to control East Sparta. The lower one, "2," operates the switch. "N," or normal, lines the switch for the main and "R," or reverse, lines it for the passing siding. The middle lever, "1," displays an eastbound signal when thrown to the left and westbound, to the right.

22 This is the Sparta Junction towerman's desk, controlling a bank of 21 levers. The center set operates switches; the sets to the left and right operate the westward and eastward signals, respectively. A manipulation chart on the desk shows the order in which to operate switch and signal levers.

interlocking by interlocking, allowing for operators with a modeled interlocking plant and levers or grips to replicate the working parts of the prototype, **14**.

Second, we can use the input data and the constraints of the system to build logic and custom-build or custom-manufacture an actual Centralized Traffic Control panel using replica or actual parts from the prototype to build a working machine, **15**. For major railroads set in the 1950s through the 1980s, this is a worthy project, although one that requires a large investment in equipment, time,

and effort.

Centralized Traffic Control machines are beautiful but complicated; you should be aware that on the prototype they relied on entire departments of technical experts for maintenance, **16**. Like the prototype, the best way for you to approach building a working CTC machine is to reach out to the experts who are familiar with the incredible project of building—and maintaining—a working CTC machine.

Third, we can use the input data and constraints as before to build a working CTC panel or screen on a computer.

Computerized CTC machines came into broad use in the 1970s to replace the original maintenance-intensive relay-based CTC machines. By 1990, the relay-based CTC machine was rare, and microprocessors increasingly replaced the old relay-based equipment in the dispatching office and in the signaling equipment in the field.

On today's railroads, computer-based CTC is the dominant form of control in signaled territory, and microprocessor equipment in the field has replaced almost all relay-based equipment.

For this series of choices, and a

23 Signals here at East Sparta Interlocking on Jerry Dziedzic's Lehigh & Hudson River main line are controlled by Signals By Spreadsheet (SBS) software. The software drives matching SBS hardware, in this case Distributed Input/Output (DIO) boards, to display aspects. Jerry models the New York, Susquehanna & Western, but including the L&HR allows for signaled interlockings to be part of his layout.

Just what is this C/MRI anyway?

C/MRI stands for Computer Model Railroad Interface. It is a system wherein a set of electronic modules allows a computer, using its serial port, to monitor and control real world devices, specifically (in our case) items on our model railroad. This includes signals of all types, track switches, occupancy detection, staging track matrixes, CTC control systems, tower control and any type of signal system so desired (CTC, ABS, APB, etc.) History has so far proven that there is very little C/MRI cannot control—you can even rig it up to turn on the blender for your favorite after-session cocktail if so desired!

The system was first introduced by Dr. Bruce Chubb in 1985 in a series of articles in *Model Railroader* magazine and has since spread throughout the hobby, being featured in countless more articles and books. A refresher series of articles featuring many new additions and updates to the system was published (again in MR) starting in January 2004. Bruce's own large pioneering layout (The Sunset Valley Oregon System) continues to be a stunning example of the flexibility, power, efficiency and tremendous versatility of the concept. Bruce has also published five books on the subject, including a Users Manual and Applications Handbook (in several versions), as well as manufacturing electronic boards and hardware to enable folks who do not wish to create their own boards. All of this is marketed through Bruce's company, JLC Enterprises (jlcenterprises.net).

C/MRI continues to be a huge success and has greatly simplified the design, control, wiring and programing of signal systems, its most common use. It is the most renowned totally universal input/output (I/O) system, designed to work with every computer and every model railroad to meet every need. With over 3,000 layouts currently using the system, there is almost always someone who has experience with it or knowledge of its functionality. This is critically important for those of us who are not electronic experts and know nothing of computer programming—having someone nearby or on your crew who knows this system is a great aid. There is a C/MRI chat group out there that provides support as well. Regardless, documentation on the

One of the handy things about C/MRI is the ability to spread the nodes around the layout to reduce wiring. This photo of Steve Mallery's PRR Buffalo Line layout shows eight mini nodes located together (plus the telephone punch block system to maintain clean and neat wiring practice), which is for the CTC machine itself. The small card on the lower right is a RS232 to RS485 conversion card, where the code line from the computer terminates. There are nine additional nodes scattered around the layout. *Phil Monat*

system as well as its abundant applications is widespread and exceptional. There is no end of computer folks or inventive modelers who have figured out yet another special thing that can be done with C/MRI.

How the system functions electronically is not for discussion here, I suggest you visit Bruce's website and read further, but it isn't all that complex. The basic concept, however, is to distribute input/output nodes around your layout, whereby each of your railroad devices that you want to interface, such as wayside signals, track occupancy detectors, switch motors, panel switches, pushbuttons, turnout position indications and panel LED lights, simply connect to the appropriate input or output pins on the nearest node.

The nodes can be located anywhere, but being able to put them right at junctions, yards, control panels, or other areas of intense activity shortens field wiring needs. Up to 128 nodes are possible and the only connection between the nodes is a single four-wire shielded cable that daisy-chains from node to node. The computer is at the end of this cable where it plugs into the serial port. The point here is you do not need thousands and thousands of wires running to your CTC machine, tower panel or relays and hardwired boards, a great savings in time, effort and money.

While the hardware and wiring side of

the system is loosely described above, the real fun begins when you get into the computer. Writing computer code is a skill most of us do not have, but it really isn't that difficult and in truth, there are lots of people who really enjoy this part of the hobby.

The computer scans the electronics on the layout and translates all of those on/off and in/out pins into commands to the signals, switch motors and LED lights all over the layout. It does this because it is running a program you wrote (often in Visual Basic or other programming languages) that delineates your layout. If you happen to have a CTC panel or you're sitting in a tower controlling a junction, when you reach out and throw a switch lever and pull up a signal to authorize authority for a train to move, the computer reads the state of the layout, decides if it's safe and appropriate for such a move, sends control data out onto the layout to enable said move, and then tells you when it has confirmation that your commands have been accomplished. And all of this in less than a blink of an eye. It is running that critical program you (or your friend) wrote, which is the real operational heart of your system.

Writing your program for any software-based system often scares many folks as it is a skill foreign to most of us, but in truth it is truly fun to learn. It is also important to note that the JMRI free-ware often used for programming Digital Command Control (DCC) decoders can also be used to set up similar controls of the C/MRI that one would do with a language-based program, such as the above mentioned Visual Basic. This also has the advantage of being portable across all types of computers including the Rasberry PI, Linux, Apple iOS and Windows PC.

Visual Basic has been around for over five decades now and is very easy to learn. Someone who has professional skill or a desire to use something more complex can certainly do that, but the point is that instead of having banks of relays, miles of wiring in countless colors and bundles, electronic boards that are hard-wired and systems that are ridged and inflexible, with this approach you have a computer program that you can easily alter, expand, change and adapt to your layout. Once you get that signal, switch, LED or other device (whatever it may be) out on the layout into the computer, you can manipulate and control it anyway you desire.

The C/MRI system is designed for the hobbyist and primarily for the Do-It-

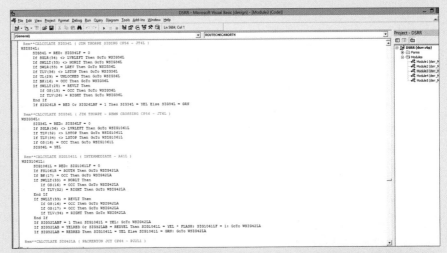

This screenshot shows a single page of a very small section of the code program, written in Visual Basic, which is a language-based computer code. This section controls some of the signals at CP 56 (Jim Thorpe) and the crossing with the Reading Blue Mountain & Northern on Phil's layout. The term "language based" means just that—it is in English and relatively easy to understand once you learn the tricks of the language. *Phil Monat*

Yourselfer with the goals of being easy to understand, assemble, test, install, maintain and expand. It is easy to apply, robust, economical and completed tested (if you choose to purchase the components fully assembled) or you can lower your costs further by purchasing kits. Bruce has done

a wonderful job of supporting his system, and there are so many users of it now that it is truly universal across the hobby. If you are planning or wish to build a layout with working signals, automation, or complex controls, C/MRI should certainly be considered.—*Phil Monat*

This photo of Phil Monat's CTC machine and desk area shows two computers. The one on the right is running the C/MRI code written in Visual Basic by Phil's good friend and programmer Bill Carr, while the other machine in the center supports JMRI/DecoderPro as well as the WiFi for throttle control. Whenever Phil wants to make a change on the layout, alter a signal aspect, change a time restraint or anything else, he just sits at the desk and types away (with his friend Bill's help!). Additional features for CTC programing via C/MRI include Route Locking, Fleeting, OS Bell activation, Maintainer Call, APB signaling, a variety of local control for turnouts, electric locks, Traffic Lever support and automated Foreign road traffic crossing generation. *Phil Monat*

The New York Central operator at Mifflin, Ohio, has lined a route out of the siding on the Maumee across the New York Central diamonds for Maumee train No. 20. The crew sees the semaphore blade move from horizontal (stop) to diagonal, an aspect that describes a rule in the Maumee rulebook. That rule gives the indication, the information needed by the crew to run their train. *Bill Darnaby*

Maumee Mikado no. 498 rumbles through the diamonds with the Pennsylvania RR at Sciotovale, Ohio, with the PRR's distinctive position lights guarding the interlocking. Pennsylvania RR controls this route and Maumee trains must approach the interlocking prepared to stop. *Bill Darnaby*

choice of anyone modeling working signals after about 1980, the computerized control is a good choice. By that date, the prototypes were leaning toward computer control with many having already made the change as dispatcher offices consolidated and towers closed.

For modelers, there are a number of resources available for the programming and construction of the software, and most of them are approachable enough to allow the aspiring builder to do much of the work him/herself. Like any CTC, computer control can be complicated, but available software like JMRI (Java Model Railroad Interface, available free at jmri.org) and Crandic Automated Traffic System (CATS) allows some efficiency in getting up and running as

we will see in Chapters 7 and 8, **17**.

So, which way do you go? What is the best solution for your layout? We'll take a look at a few examples to round out your vision and direction into the next few chapters.

Classic Interlocking Control

Early in the days of signaling, once railroads realized the benefits, changes came quickly but implementation was phased in over time, **18**. This allowed systems to develop safe operating procedures while still moving the traffic during construction.

In those times, interviews with tower operators have provided a clue into the methodology: each tower was connected by telegraph, and each had a unique call sign. As a train passed a tower, the tower operator or station agent would record the passage of that train on a written record of train movements. These records were typically large printed sheets so that each record was dubbed an "OS" report—short for "On Sheet."

Each entry showed which train had passed that point, when and in which direction. This nomenclature was common across railroads east and west, north and south. Operators on the PRR, NYC, Santa Fe, SP, etc. would follow the same basic procedures subject to their home railroad rules and common practice.

As manual interlockings were installed, there was effectively a sort of "Manual Traffic Control" where the operator or his or her designee at each tower would then reach out to the next tower, advising them of what was coming their way. Timetables were central to this sort of operation and provided authority to most of the trains over the route. Extras had to avoid trains listed in the timetable.

Signals at each manual interlocking allowed trains to pass through that interlocking, but not without written authority in the form of the timetable or a train order. As the train approached the next tower down the line, that operator too would "OS" a train movement and let the dispatcher and next tower know, and so forth. As the dispatcher tracked movements on

Miami Junction on Bill Darnaby's Maumee Route is modeled as a New York Central mechanical interlocking where the Maumee crosses the "Big Four" route of the NYC. Bill used an NYC prototype for his tower including all the linkage for switches and signals. *Bill Darnaby*

the system through the OS reports, he or she could make decisions on where to hold certain trains for meets or where to hold one for another superior or priority movement as well.

The dispatcher would then reach out to the tower via telegraph as needed to direct routes to be set accordingly and for the appropriate signal aspects to be displayed. The telegraph communication between the towers, agents and dispatchers, along with the new interlocking hardware at each location where the trains would change routes, created a new level of efficiency and safety. Later, telegraphs were supplemented by telephones and wayside phones on a "block line"—a party line between stations, towers and the dispatcher's office that allowed communication without disturbing the dispatcher. Again the bar on safety and efficiency was raised, **19.**

Manual interlockings can

Chesapeake & Ohio coal empties slide through the interlocking at Gastonia, Ohio, and the diamonds with the Maumee Route. Chesapeake & Ohio's distinctive cantilever signals guard its main tracks, with mast signals protecting the Maumee. Maumee trains approach this interlocking prepared to stop. Control here is via CTC, with a beautiful replica machine visible on the desk below the fascia. If an operator is on duty, they will authorize movement by lining the route for approaching trains; if no operator is on duty then Maumee crews act as a surrogate C&O operator and line the routes themselves before crossing the diamonds. *Bill Darnaby*

At Beech City, Ohio, Bill Darnaby's Maumee Route crosses the Erie's line between Dayton and Marion, Ohio. Erie controls the plant, and has given its local precedence over the Maumee's train. Once the Erie train clears, the operator will use the armstrong levers at right to line its route and signals. *Bill Darnaby*

be simulated using towers and interlockings along with a block line. Manual interlockings, whether lever-and-rod operated (aka "armstrong"), electrical, electromechanical, or pneumatic, were common through the 20th century in the United States and many lasted well into the 1990s, especially in complex terminal areas where individual railroads had less motivation to pay their share of the upgrade to a computerized interlocking.

Depending on prototype, interlocking switches and signals were controlled by levers, handles, or "pistol" grips, which can be modeled in a variety of ways we will discuss as we get into the details. In many cases it is prototypical for a tower operator to control his/her own interlocking and several adjacent plants through remote-control installations and several layouts do just that.

Triple action at Allegheny on Ted Pamprin's beautiful Chesapeake & Ohio: Allegheny no. 1601 takes a spin while a local shoves east into the controlled siding by signal indication, and a westbound time freight enters the interlocking. Signals allow for dynamic action and flexible operation.

HO Tower

Interlocking towers fascinated me long before my first driver's license, when bike rides to Erie Lackawanna's Ridgewood Junction got me into foreign territory, 5 miles away from home. There, a classic Erie tower lorded over a four-track main, sending commuter trains down one of two routes toward New York City.

A few years later, I summoned the courage to march up the steps of another Erie Lackawanna tower, Newburgh Junction, measuring them carefully so I could tumble down safely when I was thrown out. Instead, the operator received me warmly, explaining mysterious bells and winking panel lights while relays thunked away.

One by one, towers fell to CTC and closed. I jumped at the opportunity when Henry Freeman proposed a railfan trip to Baltimore & Ohio's Sand Patch grade in 2007 and arranged an unofficial visit to HO Tower in Hancock, W.Va.

HO was one of B&O's last. Z Tower in Keyser, W.Va closed shortly before our visit. HO had only weeks remaining when we arrived, leaving the tower in Brunswick, Md. the sole survivor. HO guarded a small yard and the junction of the Berkeley Springs branch, which still loaded out respectable sand tonnage. HO tower had special appeal to me because it was a mechanical interlocking, an armstrong plant complete with pipe rodding and bell cranks. We watched as Larry Lee, the operator who received us, handled six trains through the plant, throwing levers as easily as flicking at a fly. When he invited us to try during a lull in the action, we showed how little we understood about the efficient movement of the human body. I have a vivid memory, exaggerated only a little, of the levers throwing Jim Schweitzer like a dog shaking a Raggedy Ann doll. My own efforts were as miserable as Jim's: lesson, stomp on that pedal while squeezing the release ratchet and heave the lever (and what must have been a mile of rusty pipe connecting it to switch points) into place.

The next stop in our itinerary beckoned. We moved on, but never so far for me to forget such a once-in-a-lifetime memory.—
Jerry Dziedzic

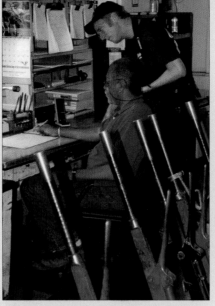

Larry Lee, the operator on duty, shows visiting Jim Schweitzer entries on the tower's block record.

Jim demonstrates how an armstrong plant earned its name.

Hancock's model board shows a track diagram pierced with illuminated panel lights and labeled with switch and signal numbers. Six General Railway Signal rotary switch handles stretch across the bottom row of the panel, apparent modifications to the original interlocking bed.

CSXT 2213, a road slug, threads through the interlocking at HO Tower on May 1, 2007. Note the intricate rodding leading from the tower to distant switches.

28 This is the operator's desk at A Tower on Ted Pamperin's Chesapeake & Ohio. The CTC panel controls the switches and signals at Allegheny interlocking, while the board on the left operates the train-order signals at stations across the railroad. A small video screen looks out the window of the tower on the layout, giving the operator a visual cue.

You can model this approach in several ways. Jerry Dziedzic, who writes the monthly "On Operation" column for *Model Railroader* magazine, modeled his version of Sparta Junction on the Lehigh & Hudson River Railway (L&HR) and the New York, Susquehanna & Western Railroad (NYS&W) in New Jersey as an armstrong plant. Sparta Junction was a diamond between the NYS&W and L&HR. Jerry has adapted the prototype Sparta Junction for his purposes, replacing the diamond with a crossover arrangement and adding a tower controlled by NYS&W to allow for Lehigh & New England trackage rights trains on NYS&W to safely funnel onto the L&HR , **20**. Jerry has even included the far end of the local passing siding on the L&HR as a remote-controlled interlocking named East Sparta, **21**. Jerry only models these two interlockings, both controlled by the Sparta Junction operator, but the

29 Home signals for westbound trains at MX cabin, Hinton, W.Va., guard the interlocking limits. Space considerations required Ted to extend yard leads through the interlocking, and the red-over-yellow "restricting" aspect is displayed for yard movement on the right.

setup would be conducive to more interlockings as well.

Jerry designed a system that simulates an armstrong-style interlocking as discussed in Chapter 1. The towerman at SJ operates switch and signal levers in an exact order to route a train through the interlocking. Nothing but stops would display if he chose the wrong lever, delaying any train waiting for a signal, **22**. More modern systems relieved the towerman of this, relying on electrical relays to determine which signal aspect to display.

Jerry's signals rely on Process Automation & Integration's "Signals by Spreadsheet" software, hosted by a personal computer running Windows 7. He used Hump Yard Purveyance levers, which resemble armstrong installations. The levers operate small slide switches that transmit normal/reverse commands to Tortoises and on/off commands to tri-color light-emitting diodes.

Input/Output (I/O) boards collect lever and switch positions, as well as block occupancy from Digital Specialties DBD-22 detectors. Jerry uses Digitrax Digital Command Control; Digitrax's integrated LocoNet carries this information to and from software and the hardware, **23**.

Jerry worked with a friend, Mike Burgett, for construction of the CTC panel for East Sparta. With a timetable-based lineup sheet for the operations in hand, the Sparta Junction operator can line routes and signals as needed for approaching trains. In this case, the lineup sheet acts like a report from a distant tower that a certain train will be approaching.

Bill Darnaby uses several different control systems for interlockings on his layout. His Maumee Route is a freelanced road running across the Midwest, and the layout showcases trackage in Ohio featuring Timetable & Train Order operation and extensive scenic details.

The Maumee crosses the main lines of several railroads including the C&O, NYC and PRR, to name a few, **24**. Simulated armstrong levers are the control at several of his interlockings,

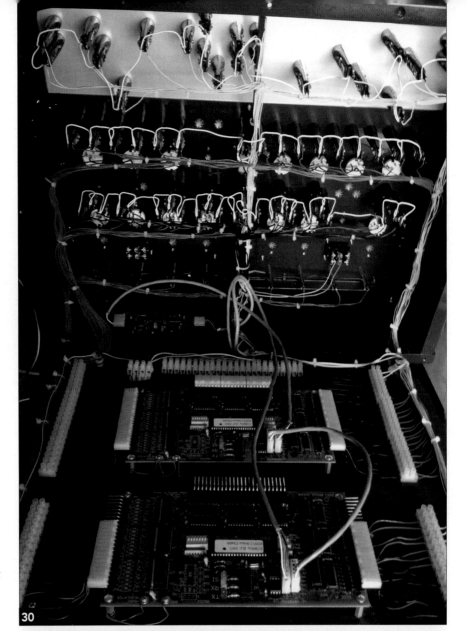

This is the wiring of Ted Pamperin's CTC panel. *Ted Pamperin*

The CTC machine in ALTO Tower, Altoona, Pa., at 10:54 p.m. on a night in February 2011. This US&S machine controls, from left to right, CP WORKS, CP ROSE, CP HOMER, and CP ANTIS on the NS Pittsburgh Line. Red lights indicate occupied track, green lights indicate a route lined by the operator using the levers and buttons below. *J. Alex Lang*

32

An SF30C leads a grain train out of Amarillo yard. The cantilever signal is the last signal on the eastward run and lets trains know when it's safe to enter the yard. The signal bridge was scratchbuilt by Steve Emerson and is based on a Santa Fe standard prototype that once stood at Dalies, N.M. The signal heads are by BLMA. *Sammy Carlile*

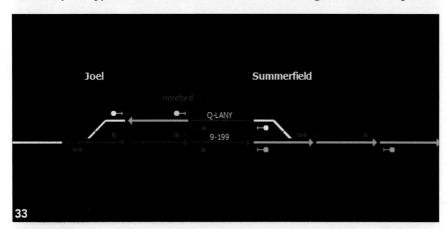

33

Farther down the route, we see a meet between two of the highest-priority trains on the ATSF in this era—the Q-LANY and the 9-199, both UPS hotshots at Hereford. This appears to be a rolling meet, always a favorite for crews. Note the green signal signifying a route lined by the DS, and the red signals opposed to them, signifying the APB automatics built into the CTC system. *Sammy Carlile*

while a CTC panel controls the crossing of his Maumee Route with the C&O at Gastonia, Ohio, **25**. The timetable requires crews running Maumee Route trains to approach different interlockings in accordance with instructions therein. Crews must take note of the signals and operate their trains accordingly.

In each case, the interlockings are equipped with the means to line the routes and turnouts. During operating sessions, if a tower operator is not on duty at an interlocking and a Maumee

crew comes to a stop signal, they must stop their train, line themselves through the plant using the simulated armstrong levers or a CTC machine, and pull up a signal route for their movement, **26**.

Bill has these controls attached to Digitrax SE8c signal controllers that use the lever or CTC-machine inputs along with detection to display signals across the interlocking. He selected Railroad & Company software in a Windows laptop for the logic on all of the interlockings and for his section

of APB/ABS on the main track. Unlocking the plant, lining switches and displaying signals is a very satisfying experience on the Maumee!

Another approach is used by Ted Pamperin on his beautifully built Chesapeake & Ohio New River Subdivision, set in 1943, **27**. In that era, the C&O had already installed CTC on parts of the road including at Allegheny, the summit of the eastern Continental Divide and a major gravitational hurdle for the C&O.

Ted faithfully models the Allegheny board, and his operator runs the board in conjunction with the dispatcher who receives OS reports from adjacent interlockings, **28**. Ted has several towers on each side of Allegheny, but since they are not manned on the layout, movement is lined by crews after authorization from the dispatcher, **29**. Ted uses C/MRI successfully on his route, including detection, signal logic, signal control, and CTC interface, **30**.

Centralized Traffic Control

Phil Monat takes the CTC to another level by dispatching the entire main line on his Delaware & Susquehanna layout from a large custom-built CTC machine (see the photo in the sidebar "What is this

C/MRI anyway?" on page 45). Compare that machine with the prototype shown in **31** at ALTO and Tony Koester's machine in **15**. Phil uses C/MRI, with some custom boards as well. The machine is in a room adjacent to the main layout room and is a beautiful adaptation of the prototype. The D&S has a single-track main line with numerous passing sidings and the CTC allows the dispatcher to route and hold trains as needed to accomplish the operating goals and to ensure movements are made safely.

Sammy Carlile models the Atchison, Topeka & Santa Fe in 1995 in the heart of the "Super Fleet" era of modern red and silver "Warbonnet" paint. His railroad depicts Santa Fe's Hereford Subdivision across West Texas and eastern New Mexico including Santa Fe's classic cantilever-mounted searchlight signal systems, with signals by BLMA, Tomar and Oregon Rail Supply, **32**. He uses Digitrax for control of the trains and JMRI to control the signal logic.

Instead of individual block detection with resistor wheelsets, he uses Circuitron rolling stock detectors and photocells for detection. There are several of the photocells between the rails in each block and the detectors report occupancy back to the Digitrax SEC8 cards. His dispatcher works off of a computer screen, much like the prototype Santa Fe did in 1995, **33**.

Sammy's system is enhanced by another software program called CATS that uses NCE, Digitrax and JMRI for data, hardware, and software architecture, but allows for a Windows-based PC controller to build a working signal system and control screen with little or no programming needed.

For my Conrail Onondaga Cutoff, set in 1994, we use NCE Digital Command Control for train control and NCE's cost-effective and robust BD20 detector for current-based detection. However, we too use Digitrax and its LocoNet command bus to drive the signal logic, turnout control, and to display aspects.

This is the power of the JMRI system: it has the ability to talk to both NCE and Digitrax simultaneously while handling the logic defined by the CATS software and driving control in the field, **34**. In a world where you have to choose a DCC system with all its proprietary components, it is refreshing and enabling to have software that allows combining the best of both worlds into a finished package. The era of 1994 allows the control to be displayed on a simple computer monitor, using the mouse to line routes and pull up aspects.

You can see there are many options for you to think about, and to pursue. Each of these are good fits for the layouts they signal, and for the layout owner who designed the system and enjoys seeing the results. All of them are complicated and require a commitment and some investment, but all are attainable by approaching the design and construction in a layered, systematic manner. Let's take a sharp look at the first step in the next chapter.

34

Conrail TV-6 tops the grade at Rams Gulch on the Onondaga Cutoff, with the city of Syracuse, N.Y., on the horizon.

CHAPTER THREE

Getting started with a manual signal system

Using manual signals during operations is one of the best ways to analyze your interlockings under traffic, and make decisions on final alignment and interlocking limits. Conrail train ELSE comes east through CP 282 early in 2013 during layout construction.

Whew! That is a lot of information so far and we are just getting started. This chapter offers more action to the prospective signal modeler. It's time to take some of the understanding and planning and start to apply all that to situations on the layout.

Right off the bat, we have more questions: How can we determine where signals should be planted along our railroad, **1**? After all, this is the most visible part of the system and given the amount of effort required to install a signal system, it is not something we want to do before being certain, **2**.

Like a roadway intersection, however, there are different options for how we lay things out, and therein lies our challenge. A step that was taken on the Onondaga Cutoff was to operate trains across the railroad using a simple paper mock-up system of manual signals to denote the interlocking limits and to provide for some operational control. This approach was also used by Bruce Carpenter and published in the April 2017 *Model Railroader*. While your layout will be different, the basics are the same across almost all interlockings.

"Wait a minute here," you may say. "Anyone can make some paper signals and pretend it's a system—I want REAL signals, not fake ones." Let's consider a few things as frame of reference: first, you're about to spend many hours and hundreds of dollars or more to accomplish something truly incredible. You're excited to move forward and to get some signal heads lit on your railroad and start to work toward the goal of a working system.

Think of the manual paper signals as a three-dimensional "artist's rendering" of your system. The rendering should be simple and cost-effective but deliver the general essence of the plan.

This is part of the key point to remember the metaphor for layers: a working system is something built on a firm foundation and that foundation is irreplaceable. You will save yourself many hours of frustration if you take the time to develop a system from the ground up and to learn lessons about how signals will affect your train movements. Let's see how a manual signal system can help you get started.

On the prototype, limits are determined by the space needed for aligning routes via turnouts in the space available to achieve operational

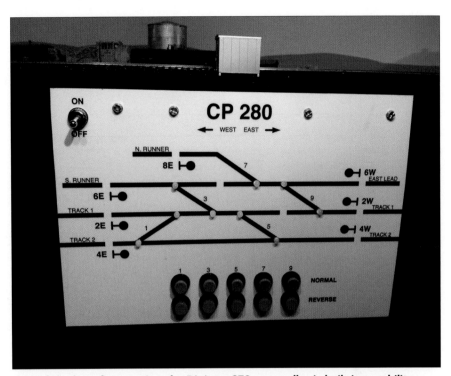

One of the benefits to using the Digitrax SE8c controller is built-in capability for local control via pushbuttons on the fascia. On the Onondaga Cutoff, I used photos of the actual local control panels in signal bungalows to design panels for the layout. Once I had the artwork drawn, I had panels custom-painted on aluminum at a local sign shop and used momentary-on pushbuttons from Miniatronics for control.

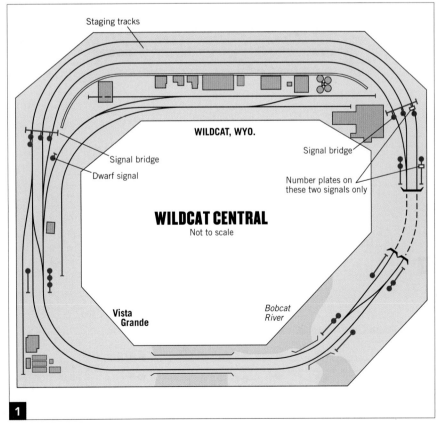

This plan from the July 2002 issue of *Model Railroader* shows likely signal locations for the Wildcat Central track plan drawn by Jim Kelly for the January 2001 MR.

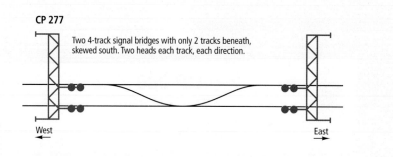

CP 277

Two 4-track signal bridges with only 2 tracks beneath, skewed south. Two heads each track, each direction.

West ←   East →

CP 280

One 2-track bridge, converted from 4-track bridge, two heads each track. One bracket mast with track 2 heads higher than track 1 heads, three heads each track. Two 2-head dwarfs, one 1-head dwarf.

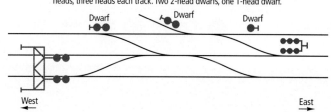

Dwarf   Dwarf   Dwarf

West ←   East →

CP 282

Two 4-track bridges: one with both tracks to south side, three heads each track; one with signals for three south tracks, two heads each track; One 3-head mast; One 2-head dwarf; one 1-head dwarf

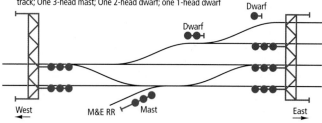

Dwarf

Dwarf

West ←   M&E RR   Mast   East →

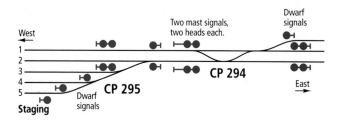

West ←

Two mast signals, two heads each.

Dwarf signals

1
2
3
4
5

CP 295   **CP 294**

Dwarf signals

Staging

East →

2

goals. The larger the interlocking, the more complicated and larger the limits will be, **3**.

These signals that guard the entrance to the interlocking are called "home signals" and govern movement into the interlocking. Each track entering the interlocking will need its own home signal. These can be located all at the same point, or can be staggered as each track approaches the first turnout in the plant.

One beauty of a manual signal system is that it allows you to develop a basic understanding of how the interlocking will look and function, including locations for your insulated joints and installing signals, without the expense of purchasing signals, wiring, and control boards.

Essentially, the manual or paper approach allows you to make changes and adjustments, and to discuss your particular setup as you get more comfortable with the concepts, **4**. Mistakes in locating manual signals are simple to rectify, especially as compared to actual working signals, since moving a working signal generally requires rewiring that signal.

For example, on the Onondaga Cutoff, significant changes were made to several interlockings after a few nights of operating trains with friends. Jack Trabachino, lifelong friend and rail-planning mastermind, acted as dispatcher by walking around the layout, deciding what would run where, lining the routes and displaying the manual signals.

Several days later he advised we needed to add a new crossover within the limits of CP 294, as well as change the limits of that interlocking and the limits up at CP 282. With manual signals, that simply meant drilling

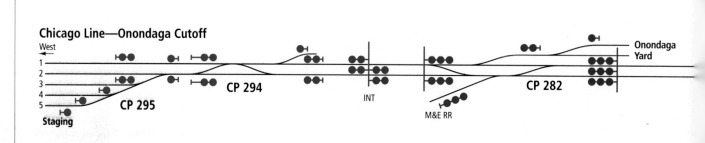

Chicago Line—Onondaga Cutoff

West ←

1
2
3
4
5

Staging

CP 295   **CP 294**   INT   M&E RR   **CP 282**

Onondaga Yard

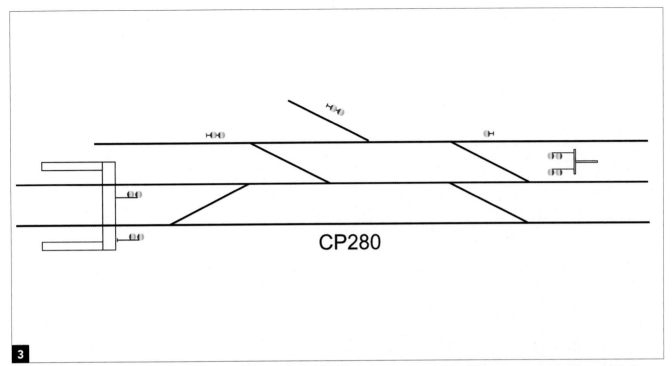

3

some new holes in the subroadbed after installing the new switches. It was additional work, but far less than would be required to move scale brass signals and redo their wiring!

Jack also recommended installing controlled signals and powering the turnouts at each end of the staging yard. We had originally designed those as manual, lined by crews as needed. The manual signal system allowed Jack to see the benefit of these being part of the controlled system in the future, **5**. Just as the prototype learns from planning and experience, including adding track and turnouts as needed, your plan will grow as you experiment and learn, **6**.

David Olesen, who models CSXT's early years on the former C&O Allegheny Subdivision, is in the process of designing and installing his signal system. His long term goal had

Manual signals allow for extra time to plan what colors or aspects are needed where, as Dave did with Integrated Signal Systems on this simple diagram for CP 282 on the Onondaga Cutoff.

4

Manual signals guard the interlocking at CP 282 on the Onondaga Cutoff. The low cost of these signals makes them ideal to move as needed to determine their best locations.

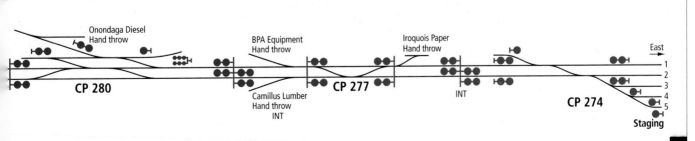

5

6 The automatic signals atop the grade on Conrail's former Lehigh Valley line through western New Jersey reflect the story to come. These are the distant signals for CP West Portal, some 2 miles distant. Train ALSE (Allentown, Pa., to Selkirk, N.Y.) slowly rolls east on the controlled siding, waiting for a meet with westbound Mail-3. The green signal on the main track reflects the fact that the Lehigh Line dispatcher has cleared a route west now that ALSE is safely in the siding. A new switch is under construction as part of the capital project to single-track the tunnel, allowing for a center track with improved clearances for future double stack and autorack trains. *Jack Trabachino*

7

Allegheny Summit on David Olesen's CSX Allegheny Subdivision is the crest of the main line, and heavy eastbounds require a push from the base of the grade near Ronceverte, W.Va., to Allegheny. Here a pair of former Chessie System SD50s have finished their push, and are descending after cutting away. In TT&TO, routing a train around them would be a cumbersome effort. With manual signals, we can test the location for needed aspects and see the result on the operation.

always been to replicate operations on one of his favorite stretches of railroad, and that would include intensive mainline operations on a coal-heavy, mountain railroad.

He had extensive familiarity with Timetable & Train Order (TT&TO) operations, and so once the track was in place and an operating scheme developed, David was up and running. Early operating sessions were successful using TT&TO clearance cards and orders for the numerous extras on the railroad and a timetable based on CSX operations in the region in the 1980s. Trains moved and the railroad came to life. Crews with clearance cards and orders would check their timetable for conflicting moves, check the register to see what had run earlier, and move their train across the route.

David had put the toggle for the switches in the fascia for crews to use. Crews lined switches themselves, typical of TT&TO rules, as needed according to their orders. As sessions progressed, though, each one would begin to unravel once locals were out across the railroad, and through freights were held due to congestion ahead, often with a clear track next to them.

In TT&TO, to run "wrong main" against the usual current of traffic, every move would require a hand-written order giving that move authority to use that track. The dispatcher had to communicate that to the operator, who copied and repeated an order, then handed it to the train crew. All of that takes a great deal of time, so much so that train orders changing the operation were rarely issued. Trains waited, **7**.

While enjoyable, something

was missing. Here was a mainline operation, double track with important high-priority freight and passenger trains, and important trains were sitting waiting for a written order to move. Adding to the complication was the fact that under TT&TO rules, trains in the timetable must not leave any scheduled station or location ahead of their scheduled departure.

This protects extra movements from occupying track designated for timetable trains running on their timetable authority. Scheduled trains were stopped, "waiting for time" while other trains waited behind them to return to work. Instead, important trains crossing over to stay moving while working around coal drags and locals as they would be in the prototype wasn't happening and congestion was balling up the railroad, **8**.

There were a lot of reasons for this

Red dwarf signals mark interlocking limits in Ronceverte, W.Va. Before the signals, TT&TO rules meant high-priority moves had to wait for train orders to work around congested areas.

Manual signals provide aspects for crews on David Olesen's layout. Amtrak train No. 51, the westbound *Cardinal*, is making its station stop at White Sulphur Springs, W.Va., while another coal drag comes upgrade behind a string of CSX EMDs.

10

Ronceverte, W.Va., is a small town full of big railroad action. This was a spot with frequent congestion as locals occupied main tracks while through freights had to wait. Installing manual signals allowed a main track to be held clear for through traffic, while a local operator could cross trains over around local jobs between the other movements.

congestion. In addition to waiting for time, locals had "yard limits" on the main line at each yard location so that all trains except Amtrak passenger trains ("First Class" as designated by the timetable) had to approach yard limits prepared to stop. High-priority time freights with no work were waiting for permission from a local yardmaster.

Yard Limits on main track were common on railroads that were governed by TT&TO. However, in the era David modeled on CSX, they were virtually non-existent. Piggyback and auto parts trains on the prototype C&O in the 1980s did not wait for time or for the yard crew to give permission to use the mainline track, **9**.

As time went on, David decided to give manual signals a try. After a night

or two of preparation, he deployed a simple manual system during several operating sessions to explore how his operations would work with signals as opposed to Timetable & Train Order.

He and several others walked the railroad, discussing each area with turnouts which had been built to represent interlockings and hand-throws, allowing for a tangible approach to establishing signal locations.

Signals for David's railroad were assembled from simple leftover plastic sprue from kits. Sprues were painted black near the tops, with silver masts below to suggest prototype practice, with simple colored-paper hole punches glued to the sprue to represent color signals.

These masts were created with a variety of aspects to help simulate the

prototype. Holes to fit the sprues were drilled in the layout subroadbed to accept the new masts with a friction fit. Each track on the main line received two holes at the interlocking limits. As trains moved toward the interlocking, the first hole was used for a small home mast, with one red disc. Appearing as a dwarf signal, this by itself functioned as the stop indication. By leaving it in place, the aspect could be modified by placing taller colored aspects immediately behind the first dwarf signal, **10**.

On the trial operating day, instead of the typical TT&TO operator position, the dispatcher worked with two levermen, one for each end of the railroad. Levermen acted as tower operators. When the dispatcher needed a route lined, instead of dictating

11 Manual signals indicate an occupied block ahead.

The operator lines a route and installs the "clear" signal in the hole behind the dwarf signal.

12 The crew pulls the "clear" aspect as the train passes and returns it to the storage box.

orders on the phone to the operator, he would use a Family Radio System (also known as FRS) radio to call out a route to the appropriate leverman, who would in turn line the turnouts and use the second hole to insert a second mast, this one with an aspect displayed, **11**.

In effect, the levermen would be responsible to ensure the route was clear of other trains or equipment, then insert aspects allowing permission on the proper route only. Other routes were left with just the stop signal indication on the dwarf. Any movement on those routes would need

to stop (observing the stop signal) and wait for a new aspect to be installed.

Crews running trains on the route as dictated by the dispatcher were then instructed by rule to manually remove the taller aspect mast as they passed the aspect and place it in a small bin below the layout, **12**.

The results were impressive. With control of the routes and lining of the indications in the hands of the dispatcher and levermen, operational solutions were much easier to implement than they had been before. Now, mainline moves could be routed

on either track, allowing trains to move efficiently around one another if one was stopped ahead, **13**.

Yard Limits on the main were eliminated, meaning local trains and switchers now needed to get permission of their own to occupy main track—but with the levermen watching all the movements, these moves were able to get track time as needed. Best of all was the flow of this new operation, **14**. The most important freight trains no longer were bound by the timetable or published schedule; they no longer needed to wait for time. High-priority trains could even run early as needed. This kept the main line much more fluid and in turn reduced congestion.

Manual signals were a great step for David to take. While entirely manual, the concepts of block signaling operation are consistent with more complicated electrical systems. The manual system allowed David to define interlocking limits, explore and determine where to locate the signals, and allowed his operating crew to see where those limits would be as well as how to operate following signal aspects. Likewise, it is a great place for you to begin—small steps that begin your journey to a working signal system.

BX Cabin, just west of Covington, W.Va., is where the double-track Chesapeake & Ohio main line opens up for several industrial tracks and a small yard. Here we see it at a quiet moment, red dwarf signals marking interlocking limits and showing that no route is set through the interlocking.

A few minutes later, two trains converge, but thanks to the flexibility of the manual signal system, the operator can move time freight No. 94 around the Covington Yard Job with no delay.

CHAPTER FOUR

TRAIN DETECTION: The signal system's foundation

Dynamic brakes howl as NS 236 comes downgrade at Villamont, Va., past the automatic signals on classic Norfolk & Western bracket masts. The curve to the west required the signals for eastbounds to be mounted at different elevations to maximize visibility over passing trains.

As you are setting out to install signals on your layout, it is difficult to overstate the criticality of "train detection"—the manner in which your signal system will know which track is occupied and which is not. As we discussed in earlier chapters on prototype systems, there is no path to reliable, functional signals without reliable and robust detection.

Magnetic reed switches like this one from Radio Shack are an old method for detecting block occupancy. *Larry Puckett*

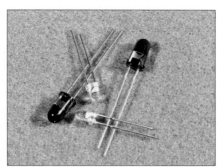

Visible-light and infrared emitters and phototransistors are very popular for some types of train detection circuits. *Larry Puckett*

The Nightscope infrared detector has an infrared emitter and detector, with an open-collector transistor switch built in. *Larry Puckett*

Phototransistors are fairly fast-acting detection sensors yet can easily fit between HO ties. *Larry Puckett*

Block occupancy detection sensors like this BD20 have no direct connection to the track bus, instead relying on coils of the track feeder bus wire to induce a sensing current.

1

The prototype calls this "track occupancy" since revenue equipment will show track as occupied; since we are designing detection systems we will refer to "detected sections." Signaling follows the same linear thinking that defines most logic and computer systems. Simply put, "garbage in equals garbage out." If the on-off data from your detection is inconsistent or unreliable, your signal system will also work inconsistently and unreliably. On the other hand, a reliable and robust detection system will lead to years of satisfying signal operations.

Using our philosophy of layers that work together to build a functional system, detection is the foundation of the system. Like the foundation of a building, everything to come later depends on this first step. Good, stable trackwork and wiring principles are critical. Once your track is in place, detected sections established with insulated joints and power supply determined, you are ready. Let's build it

right the first time to provide years of enjoyment.

The key point regarding detection is that we need some way to generate a simple on-off input, automatically and without error, so that our system can know when a track is occupied and when it is not. This simple on-off data point is the foundation of signal logic, and the input that is required so that the system will function reliably. To be clear, bulletproof detection leads to bulletproof signaling.

There are several popular methods of detection: photocell/phototransistor, reed switches, infrared, and current-based, **1**. Whether you are running a Digital Command Control (DCC) layout, DCC with Layout Command Control (LCC), or direct-current (DC), there are detectors that will work for you. Each has several manufacturers that provide equipment for the task.

Photo-detection is a method that uses photocells or, if built today,

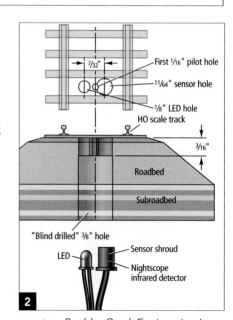

2

courtesy Boulder Creek Engineering Inc.

Wiring Principles

Signaling, like many animated features of a layout, demands extra wiring beyond track power. Even when a DCC or LCC bus will carry track, switch and signal information, it must be wired into the local hardware. It follows that good wiring techniques are essential in constructing a signal system. At the very least, wire identification (whether by color coding or other labeling system) must be uniform with bus wires labeled in some manner to aid you in keeping your system straight. Inevitable mistakes are much more easily deciphered when you can refer to your labels, installed as you go along.

Long wire runs should be drawn gently through holes or hangers in the benchwork that allow the bus to remain close to the track, but in an organized manner. Joints between bus wires and terminals should be made via terminal strips. Joints between feeder wires and the bus should be with suitcase clamp-style connectors or, even better, soldered directly to the bus. (The Onondaga Cutoff was overbuilt with solid-core 12-gauge bus wire and 20-gauge feeders soldered to each and every separate piece of rail on the entire layout. Tony Koester's Nickel Plate takes that even further: 10-gauge buses and 18-gauge feeders!) Remember—it is easier to do it right the first time, and depend on it forever, than to have to go back and find the one loose suitcase connector amongst thousands.

Good wiring technique is especially critical on the prototype, too.

Nick Anshant

J. Alex Lang is building a Conrail layout to represent his memories of Conrail in the Bethlehem, Pa., area in 1994. As seen here his wiring is off to a good start. Note consistent color coding of wires and organization of boards.

J. Alex Lang

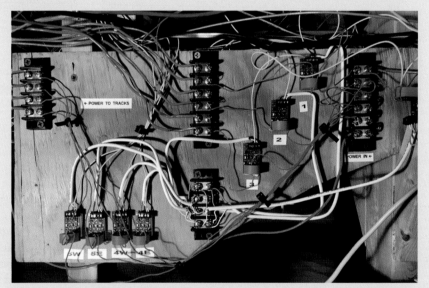

This is the block detection panel for the staging yard on the Onondaga Cutoff. Clear, bold labeling helps identify the components for maintenance and troubleshooting. The power bus from the breakers enters the panel from the right and is distributed across a terminal strip. From that terminal strip, 22-gauge wires take the power to a series of eight BD20 block detection boards, with varying numbers of passes through the "tombstone." The power then goes to the two other terminal strips and out to the track. Each BD20 is wired with power cables (the white two-conductor cable) and a yellow wire that takes the on-off output to the AIU, which communicates to the system.

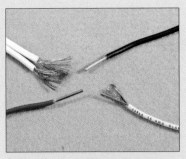

Solid wire is stiff and doesn't flex very well, but it's good for heavy power buses. Stranded wire is made up of multiple small wires and is flexible, making it a good choice for wires that will be moved a lot. *Larry Puckett*

Terminal strips and terminal blocks allow for quick and easy screw connections. *Larry Puckett*

Depending on the code of your track, install power feeders every 3 to 6 feet— use more feeders for smaller rail.

3-6 feet

Heavy power bus wires follow track under layout

Small feeder wires connect each section of rail to power bus wires under layout

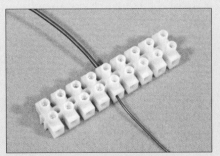

Terminal blocks are great for connecting two wires of different sizes together. The screws provide a strong grip on the wires. *Larry Puckett*

Screw terminals can be used with individual wires or with a jumper to connect to multiple wires. *Larry Puckett*

Crimped spade connectors make for fast and neat installations. *Larry Puckett*

phototransistors or similar apparatus mounted in the track. Normally the switch senses light and is in an open status. When equipment passes over, the switch senses shadow and closes. This creates the simple on-off data needed for signal logic. These outputs are then fed back to the input terminals on the signal decoder or input card for the computer to indicate track occupancy. This system is most effective for a single-level layout with bright lighting. Dark areas, double-deck layouts, or layouts that operate with the lights turned down low make these switches less effective.

Reed switches are magnetic switches that were commonly used on layouts before the easy availability of photocell, phototransistor, or infrared receivers. Reed switches have a spring and magnet inside, and magnets mounted on the bottom of passing equipment cause the switch to throw. Given the mechanical nature and the need to install magnets on equipment, however, this method is not as popular today as it once was.

A more widely reliable method is infrared detection, available from several manufacturers including Azatrax, Signalogic, and others. Commonly used for stand-alone accessories such as grade-crossing gate sensors or for one stand-alone block signal, infrared detection uses light-emitting diodes (LEDs) paired with a receiver, **2**. The LED generates light in the infrared spectrum, invisible to human eyes, and the receiver is designed to "see" only that light.

It requires no modification of equipment. Configurations from different firms may vary, but again in all cases the "on-off" nature of the track circuit is replicated for our purposes. Infrared detectors can be set up with the LED and receiver across from each other on the track or, alternatively and more reliably, between the rails if installed so as to be reflective off the bottom of passing equipment.

One advantage of these systems is that no insulated rail joints are required for the signal system. The effectiveness of them is more suited for

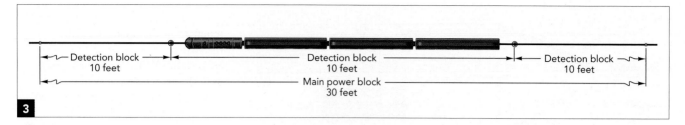

Detection block
10 feet

Detection block
10 feet

Detection block
10 feet

Main power block
30 feet

3

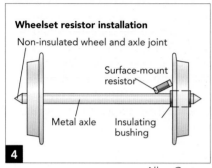

Wheelset resistor installation

Non-insulated wheel and axle joint

Surface-mount resistor

Metal axle

Insulating bushing

4

Allan Gartner

detection to the simpler applications of intermediate "automatic" signals, and simple interlockings, due to several issues. First, they only detect at the location installed, instead of across an entire block. Equipment that is not over the detector will not be detected. Second, a minimum of two detectors is required, one at each end of every detected section. With infrared, the reflective setup requires drilling holes between the rails of your track or adjacent to the track according to the manufacturer's instructions to have the LED and receiver set at a 45-degree angle to the track, allowing beams to come up from the LED.

When no equipment is overhead, the sensor is "off." When any equipment passes over the track, beams reflect off passing equipment which can therefore be seen by the receiver, turning the receiver "on." No modification to rolling stock is necessary with proper adjustment of the angle and elevation of the receiver pair. The system is independent of track power and is therefore effective for battery-powered equipment (so-called "dead rail" operation) as that method of locomotion grows or for animated accessories independent of track power.

However, for a signal system application, issues arise. The fact infrared detectors show occupancy at one location only, not any location within the detected section, means

loose cars or short trains that are not triggering an infrared receiver pair will be undetected. The receiver pairs also require a minimum of four LEDs (and eight wires) per detected section.

Further, sensors are mounted in the track or roadbed, and so track must be drilled with mounting holes. Given the need for the receiver to "see" the infrared light, the sensors can be affected by dust and dirt over years. All of this can be cumbersome and becomes especially so at each and every interlocking, given the need for multiple short detected sections within interlockings and especially those that include parallel moves.

Still, even with these limitations, reed switches, photo-based, and infrared systems are most suitable for DC-powered railroads due to the fact that they operate independent of track power. Infrared allows operation in low-light situations as we have seen.

Since the voltage in the track on DC layouts necessarily changes to control your train speeds, current-based detection is not generally as reliable on DC layouts as it is on layouts controlled by DCC. Current-based detectors need power applied in the rails in order to determine if equipment is present. With infrared or phototransistors, no power to the rails is needed to determine if track is occupied. The system can "see" equipment due to the shadow overheard.

So let's talk about a third system, current-based detection. This system, like the prototype, measures current moving from one rail to the other, making it a solid choice for DCC-powered layouts where power is constantly applied to the track. For our layouts this is accomplished using a circuit equipped with a sensor that can detect when current is traveling the path. Detection modules are

manufactured by NCE, Digitrax, RR Cir-Kits, Integrated Signal Systems and others.

Each has the capability of generating the same "on-off" logic of a relay. The railroad is divided into electrically isolated sections at each location where signals will be present, as well as anywhere else as needed. Each section is wired with a different "hot" side bus, which is in turn routed through a detection module.

When the detected section is not occupied by equipment drawing power, current doesn't move across the circuit and the detection unit is off. When equipment drawing power rolls onto the detected section from either end or from a switch, the current that starts to flow to the hot rail passes through the detection unit, which causes the detection unit to trigger to "on."

Equipment, such as a locomotive, a lit passenger car or caboose, a track powered end of train device, draws currrent continuously and therefore will trigger the detection. For many modelers, this is sufficient as it marks the beginning and end of each train, **3**.

For some applications, however, another step is needed for prototypical operation of the detected-section detection and signal system. Since the detectors only switch to on when current is being drawn in a particular detected section, long freight trains with a caboose or lit car at the rear may extend far enough to "bridge" across a shorter detected section with non-conducting cars. In this case, detected sections can be beneath a train but not have conductive axles completing the circuit and in turn those detectors will not show occupancy. The occupancy will vacillate between on and off as the train moves across the location. This is called "bouncing" detection and can be an issue since detected sections that appear unoccupied are in fact occupied.

The CTC logic, seeing unoccupied detected sections, allows turnouts to be lined or signals to be displayed as though the track was empty—obviously not a good situation if the track is actually occupied.

Resistive wheelsets

The solution to this problem is to equip freight cars with one "resistive" wheelset per truck assembly, for a total of two per car—one on each end. Using large-value resistors of 3.6k, 4.5k or 10kΩ electrically linked to metal wheels on each end of the wheelset with conductive paint or ink causes a tiny amount of current (about .1ma at 10kΩ and .4ma for 3.6kΩ) to travel through each equipped wheelset.

Current comes in from the hot rail, through the wheel, through the resistor, and back through the other wheel to ground, **4**. Detection units can be adjusted to be sensitive enough to "see" that current and therefore each car will trigger the detection. Check the manufacturer's listing for each detector you use as the sensitivity and adjustments can be modified for your purposes.

An alternative to making your own resistive wheelsets is to purchase them ready-made. JB Wheelsets (jbwheelsets.com/resistor.html) and Logic Rail Technologies (logicrailtech.com/dws.htm) manufactures them in different sizes and with different resistance values.

While it is a significant commitment of time, or, for pre-made products, money, to equip each car with resistive wheelsets, the benefits justify the cost. With each car so equipped, even short detected sections beneath the train are likely to have at least one conductive wheel. Further, any car equipped with resistive wheelsets can be the last car on your train, and the system will be aware of where that falls.

This is critical for local trains without a caboose behind and for modern modelers who are not running lit cabooses. Finally, there is clear benefit in equipping your whole fleet with metal wheelsets—their added weight improves tracking and replacing

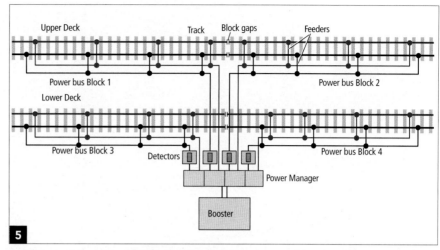

5

Double deck layouts can be organized as seen here, with power bus connections vertically up to both levels from the booster.

plastic wheelsets reduces issues with dirty track.

Regardless of the method of detection you choose, your project will require some different adaptations. Remember the concept: the system needs to know without question when equipment is and is not on a certain section of track.

Insulated joints

In order to establish detected sections from signal to signal, railroads long ago had to make provisions to electrically isolate sections of track in order for each to be considered separately in the logic puzzle of signaling. A benefit to using current-based detection is that these insulated joints are located and function much like the prototype joints within the track structure, which adds to realism and provides a template by which we modelers can proceed with signal design on the layout, **5**.

In theory, the idea is simple: any gap in the rails would insulate each side from the other; air is a good insulator. That theory is far less simple to apply on the prototype, as the wheel loadings from trains are robust. Structural stability obviously cannot be compromised for any reason. Rail joints, whether insulated or otherwise must be able to support the loadings and impact from moving trains and must remain stable in order to stay in line.

Railroads used bonded joints in jointed rail territory to improve conductivity. For insulated joints,

railroads experimented with different non-conductive materials. As the use of rubber became more common, it was incorporated—steel joint bars were dipped in or sprayed with rubber or a rubberized plastic material, which was then bolted in place to provide structural stability but to avoid electrical continuity. Even as welded rail has become common on modern main lines, insulated joints remain at all signal locations and as needed in interlockings.

Today's insulated joints are generally made in a controlled shop environment and use rubberized plastic insulation material to keep the metal parts separated. Each assembled joint includes several feet of regular stock rail on each side. Crews cut rail in the field to fit the new joint assembly, drop the entire assembly in place, and then field weld the new assembly to the existing rails in place.

Modelers have a much simpler task to install insulated joints. Several choices exist to create the insulated joints needed and they differ if your track is already in place or if you are designing your layout with detection in mind. For instance, most manufacturers of track also manufacture plastic rail joiners that can be used as needed while laying track. While effective, these can be cumbersome, and in highly-visible locations they may be unsightly as well, given their size. They are difficult to install on track that is already in place.

Insulated joints on a model railroad can be as simple as a gap cut in a rail, and filled with styrene. Details West manufactures joint bars that can be glued in place to represent the bolted joints of the prototype.

Another option is to simply cut a gap in the rails at the location of the end of the detected section using a motor tool such as a Dremel with a cut-off disc or similar rotary tool. This method works best for track already laid and glued in place. It is easiest to do this work before ballasting is installed but possible after ballasting as well, **6**.

Once the cut is made, the gap should be filled with styrene or some other plastic, which should be secured in place with cyanoacrylate adhesive. This protects against expansion or other rail movement that might bridge the gap.

Choosing a detection system

While each of the photo and infrared systems can work in certain circumstances, including DC layouts and on any layout with fairly simple interlockings, each has significant drawbacks when used for detection for more complicated interlocking arrangements. In fact, in many cases, both photo and infrared systems require necessary compromise compared to the prototype even in common applications of more complicated interlockings.

The only system that is simple enough to deliver prototype detection in complicated interlockings is a current-sensing system. These systems depend on track power and equipment that draws current and since your track must be wired regardless, they also minimize extra wiring on the layout. Current-based detection in conjunction with DCC works regardless of room lighting and has proven to be rock-solid reliable for many years on my Onondaga Cutoff as well as on many other signalized railroads.

In a current-sensing system, all current flowing to a certain detected section is routed through a detector board, where sensors are located that can determine when current is being drawn and when it is not.

Depending on the manufacturer, detectors can be located at the start of each detected section or can be located remotely at a centralized location. In any case the system must be set up so that current will be drawn through the detector. Understanding this is important to lead to understanding of the greater system and for troubleshooting later.

Since we have two long conductors in the rails, a certain tiny amount of current is always present. This is called induction and it is a physical reality in any electric system where you have parallel conductors, from high-tension power lines to model railroads.

Induction varies by length and voltage present. The longer the length and the higher the voltage, the more induction is present, and the more current flows constantly through the system. The amount of water in the air affects the system too: more humidity, more induction. For us, our detectors aren't sensitive enough to be triggered by the normal amount of induction present on our detected sections unless the detected sections are very long (more than 70 feet) or are in very high-humidity environments.

A lit passenger car or locomotive draws current, even when standing still. Lit cabooses and cars equipped with resistive wheelsets also draw current. In all these cases, the amount of current drawn is determined by that old high-school physics equation: Ohm's law.

$$i=V/R$$

Where i is the current drawn through the system measured in Amps (A);
V is the electromotive force of the system, measured in Volts (V);
R is the total resistance of the system measured in Ohms (Ω).

This can all be easily measured with a basic electrical voltmeter or ammeter, but even then it is important to understand the flows.

As an example, most DCC-equipped, sound-equipped locomotives today are relatively efficient. They may draw from about .25 amps up to .5 amps in regular operation. Some older locomotives, such as the old Athearn "blue-box" locomotives or similar, once equipped with sound, may come closer to .6 amps. These are all easily detected by most detectors. The challenge is to find the balance of making each car detectable without drawing so much power that you exceed the capacity of the DCC system circuit breakers.

Digital Command Control power is provided by a power supply in the command station along with one or more additional power boosters attached to the command station for larger layouts. From each booster, two track wires come out—hot and common. Both can run to a terminal strip, from which each separate route can be split.

Leaving the terminal strip, the next step is to run each of the buses through a circuit breaker, on the way to the track. I suggest that you install power districts on your railroad.

These clever devices electrically isolate each district, which allows most of the layout to keep running even if there is a short in one district. Further, breakers can be adjusted to allow a certain amount of current to pass before they electrically "break" the circuit, saving damage to electrical components and to your command station.

Your current needs will be determined by your equipment and plans. Longer trains, locomotives with sound, and the extra resistance of locomotives pulling upgrade all will require extra current. Most HO scale railroads, for example, need about 2-4A of current at any given time. If your requirements exceed the available capacity in your booster, you will need to add another booster or decrease your current requirements. You will have to refer to your command station's owners manual to ensure proper current allocation.

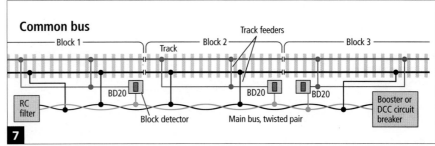

courtesy of Allan Gartner

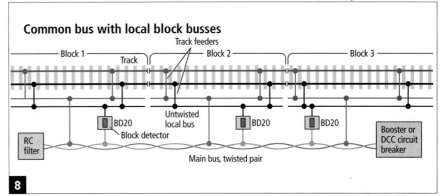

courtesy of Allan Gartner

Each BD20 (small green board, center) has an output that is wired to a channel on the NCE Auxiliary Input Unit board (large green board, right). The AIU in turn is wired into the command bus from the NCE command station, which can communicate the simple on/off status to the computer and decoders. *J. Alex Lang*

In addition to selecting and fine-tuning the breaker you need, it is time to decide how many detected sections you have to wire. This a step for careful consideration. Multiple detected sections can be wired through each breaker provided the total power requirements are less than the breaker rating.

While the common wire can be run to all districts, each separate detected section must have its own hot-side bus wire connection. All power going to

the hot rail needs to first pass through the detection unit. For every power district on your railroad, all power to the rails of that detected section must come through the detector associated with that detected section. Since the hot side is where we will be measuring current, each detected section needs its own bus. Just one feeder wire in a detected section that is mistakenly attached to the wrong bus cable or wrong track will lead to unreliable detection, which is the greatest issue

The NCE AIU has its onboard LEDs lit, indicating occupied blocks. *J. Alex Lang*

with reliable signal installation. (Yep – I learned this the hard way.)

All current to a given detected section must come through the detector for that detected section, **7**. It follows that you will need a bus for each detected section, even if they are parallel tracks: two hot bus wires for a two-track main line, three for a three-track main line, four for a four-track line, and so on, **8**. If a main and a siding, you will need a hot bus for each, plus a separate hot bus for the turnout on each end of the siding.

If you are powering your switch frogs, don't forget to include the hot leg for the frog through the detection coil. Yards and sidings that are not

signaled don't need their own bus. Remember: for signaling to work reliably, each and every separate detected section must be able to absolutely show whether or not it is occupied on a consistent basis.

For installation of each detector, we have a choice. We can locate the detector out along the line, near the spot where a detected section begins, or we can make a panel of all our detectors and run the bus cables from that panel to the detected sections. Different designs will lend themselves to different setups, and each can work—it is a matter of keeping the wire organized.

On the Onondaga Cutoff, detectors

were located at one end of the detected section they monitor, across the railroad. This was kept consistent for ease of maintenance. Follow the manufacturer's directions here. If you are using an NCE BD20-type detector or similar with the "tombstone" on the card, pass your hot bus through the tombstone, but do it with a smaller diameter stranded wire so as to allow more flexibility. On the OC, we used 20-gauge stranded wire, wrapped through the detector anywhere from 1 to 4 times depending on detected section length. For this step use stranded wire for ease of bending through the tombstone and near the soldered joints.

This close-up view shows power-in and BD-20 wiring on the Onondaga Cutoff.

This detail view shows the power-out, including BD-20s for staging tracks on the OC.

Since the BD-20s have an option to activate an indicator LED on the board, I decided to take advantage of it. Separate power adds wiring for you but allows the LEDs to work on the BD20 when it is activated, which immediately helps you identify issues with wiring, components or hardware. Once the track has power and the detector shows "on" when equipment is present on that detected section, you've completed the first step in building that first layer of your signal system, **9**.

And here, not for the first nor the last time in this book, I will stress that it is absolutely critical for you to keep track of your wiring documentation from now until you are done with your installations. You have completed your first detected section: well done!

Before you begin your next one, what is this one to be called? Like every track on the prototype, each detected section on your railroad should have a unique name or other identifier. Like the prototype, you can assign each detected section a series of numbers and/or letters that uniquely identify that particular piece of track among all others on your railroad.

There is no real magic here to how you identify detected sections—like the prototype the issue is not the method, but the fact that each detected section has a unique identifier. The prototype is your guide, but any rational system is acceptable. Remember our goal: that the system know when each detected section is occupied, **10**.

Once you see one detected section through to completion, the process becomes straightforward for every other detected section on the main line. One detector is used for each detected section regardless of length; the key again is that all power to any MUST be routed through the detector. This is to say that any and all feeders to the hot rail must stem from the bus that passes through the detector, **11**.

For long runs on larger layouts the principle remains the same, but you have some choices in execution. Use the large-gauge power bus (12- or 10-gauge wire) to run power from the booster through to the location of the detector. At that location, power can be

Testing

Once you begin, it is always tempting to keep the momentum going. Wiring can be an arduous task and one that requires many hours to install and once you wire in one feeder it can be tempting to do another and another and another. A word of caution, borne from experience: nowhere is the wiring gremlin more likely to appear than in wiring your signal system, whether it be in detection or in the signals themselves. And especially in detection, knowing quickly that you have made a mistake is by far the easiest way to undo that mistake.

As each feeder is attached, it is good practice to have a lit passenger car or lit caboose handy. If the light turns on, that track has power. But, is the power coming from the proper source? This is where it is wise after connecting each feeder to double back and check the detector and verify that it is seeing current drawn from the proper bus.

Check the detectors for adjacent detected sections, too—if they are empty, they should show no detection. If they do show detection, or if the detected section you are wiring does not, then you likely have a feeder wired to the wrong bus. I call these "crossed feeders" and they are very difficult to locate unless you test after each one is connected.

Once you have tested with a lit passenger car or caboose, it is time to check with one of your resistive wheelset-equipped cars. By design, the resistive wheelsets draw far less current than a lit car and so require a more sensitive setting on the detection unit.

While such strict regimen seems over-complicated and slow, there is good reason for this slow-and-steady approach. As things get more complicated, so do the arrangements of the detected sections. More complicated turnout arrangements add to the complexity of the detected section wiring. Consistent labeling, testing, and installation is critical to managing this complexity.

Clear, concise labeling of components is helpful during construction and especially helpful during maintenance or troubleshooting. Using terminal strips near the BD20s allows large power bus cables to be terminated so a smaller gauge wire can be used to pass through the "tombstone" for current-based block detection. *J. Alex Lang*

Resistance soldering machine:

Resistance soldering is a technique where a tool is applied to both sides of a joint, and a high current is then sent through the tool and the joint, creating hot but very local heat. Resistance soldering units are sold by several manufacturers with many features to consider. Most have adjustable voltage and come with a foot pedal for activation, very handy when using hands for the wire and solder already!

By doing preparation work for each joint and pre-tinning wire in a production-line style process, you can rapidly add feeders to the layout. Each rail location should be polished and each wire tinned ahead of time. A dab of flux is placed on the location. The wire feeder is then shaped to fit on the web of the rail, tucked into place, and the resistance soldering tool placed to touch both sides of the joint—essentially the rail and the feeder wire are sandwiched together by the resistance soldering machine tongs.

Once they are held together, a quick step on the pedal delivers the current, melting the flux. Begin with the voltage at a medium-low setting while you get the hang of it, but then feel free to play with the higher values for a quicker joint. Touch the joint with rosin-core electrical solder and with a hiss of melting flux, solder immediately should melt into the joint. Lift your foot from the pedal, release the tongs, and you have a hard clean joint that will serve well for years to come.

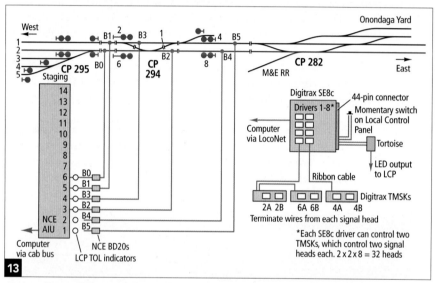

This is the system architecture and preliminary wiring diagram for CP-294.

run through a smaller-gauge stranded wire (18- or 20-gauge) to pass through the tombstone, after which it would go back to the larger gauge bus to run the length of the detected section. Feeders to the track would come from this wire only; therefore any and all power to the rails passes on this one bus and through that one detector, **12**.

When wiring detected sections, I bring a lighted passenger car or caboose with me around the railroad and I keep the feeder colors sorted with a little standard I made up. Red is the rail closest to the aisle and white is the rail farther from the aisle, unless track balloons and is in the opposite direction in the back. As you can see, there is opportunity for confusion.

Some modelers create a little traveling jig to keep this coding in mind, and others have tricks to help

them remember. What I did was set up a system whereby I would drill holes for 20 feet worth of feeders, then cut, strip and tin the feeders at the bench, assembly-line style. Each feeder would then be inserted as a "tail" into each hole, color coordinated, and once all were installed, I bent each tip. Each joint location was polished with a wire brush head on my motor tool, working from one end of the detected section to the other.

Once all locations were polished and ready, I went back to the beginning and applied a dab of electrical flux paste to each location, again from one end to the other. Starting again at one end, I finally used my resistance soldering tool to make a quick, permanent joint for each and every feeder wire in the detected section. This approach allowed me

to do production work soldering the feeders to the rails.

As I progressed on this final step of soldering the joints, after five feeder pairs or so I would go beneath the layout to attach the new feeders to the appropriate bus wire one by one. As I did this, I would place my lit passenger car on the track and turn on the track power. I could easily tell if the track had power and then I rolled the car off the detected section, making sure that all the wheels were out of the detected section, to ensure that the BD-20 then switched off. This helps to ensure not only proper wiring polarity but also that the car is not drawing power through the detected section into the next.

Now that you have the detected section wired to feeders that connect to the power bus, and you have that power bus passing through the detector unit, we can begin to wire up the detection system itself, **13**. Looking at the detection side of this system, we see the NCE BD-20 detectors linked to the NCE "Auxiliary Input Unit" (AIU).

The AIU is in turn wired into the command bus; since each AIU has a unique identifier, each of the ports on the AIU is also uniquely identified in the system, which allows us to associate each of them with track modeled in the computer. See the manufacturer's directions.

Of the four screw-terminals on a BD-20, you will have the hot and common power lead and then the wire that will run to the AIU. Again, this can be tested with our passenger car. The added benefit of the BD-20 when

14

This is a close-up view of an NCE AIU with its address set to 62, and four blocks currently occupied, as indicated by the red LEDs lit. There is no way around lots of wire—color coding and labeling are critical.

run with separate power is that the LED on the BD-20 and the LED on the AIU will both light up when the sensor is activated, allowing us to see if the system in the field is working as intended before programming starts.

Turn the track power on and roll the car into and out of the detected section. The BD-20 and the AIU input LED should both light only when the car is in the detected section, **14**.

A critical part of this process is labeling. Each BD-20 should be labeled with what detected section it protects. This can be written onto the benchwork adjacent to the card or can be taped or hung on the wires;

regardless, it is critical to know what detector is detecting what.

Each one will have a unique identifier once we enter them into the computer. So, in addition to labeling the hardware beneath the railroad, it is also critical to note which detector is attached to which input on the AIU (and which AIU it is attached to).

On smaller layouts with just a few inputs, this can seem like overkill, but even in small layouts it is easy to forget what is going on beneath the layout surface. Labeling these detected sections in the software is a critical step that will be much more likely to succeed if you keep notes on which

detector is attached to which detected section.

How does detection work within interlocking limits? The principle is the same—each detected section is isolated using insulated joints, and all hot side power to that detected section is fed through a detector unit. Instead of a length of many feet, however, interlocking detected sections are usually much shorter—sometimes in complicated interlockings consisting of just one single turnout. Essentially, from a track-circuit perspective, each interlocking is a series of short detected sections, arranged in a sequence so as to form continuous

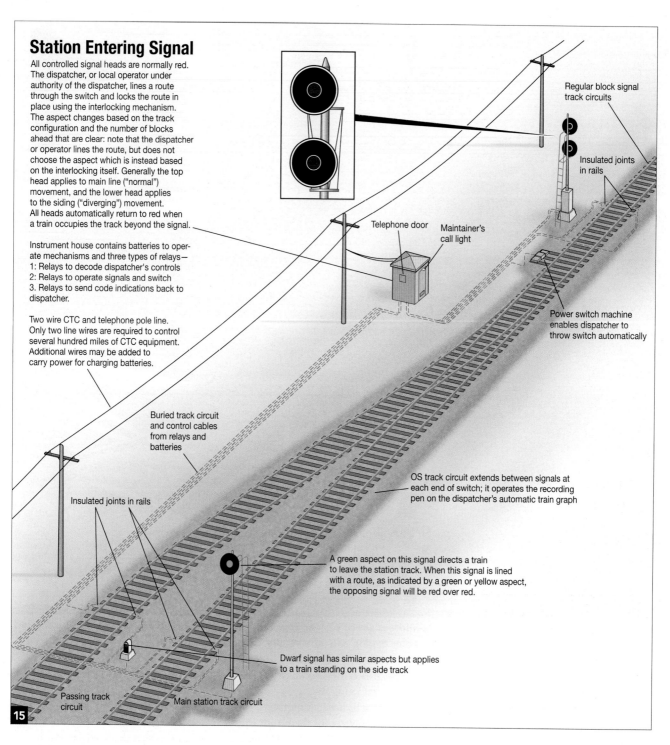

Station Entering Signal

All controlled signal heads are normally red. The dispatcher, or local operator under authority of the dispatcher, lines a route through the switch and locks the route in place using the interlocking mechanism. The aspect changes based on the track configuration and the number of blocks ahead that are clear: note that the dispatcher or operator lines the route, but does not choose the aspect which is instead based on the interlocking itself. Generally the top head applies to main line ("normal") movement, and the lower head applies to the siding ("diverging") movement. All heads automatically return to red when a train occupies the track beyond the signal.

Instrument house contains batteries to operate mechanisms and three types of relays—
1: Relays to decode dispatcher's controls
2: Relays to operate signals and switch
3. Relays to send code indications back to dispatcher.

Two wire CTC and telephone pole line. Only two line wires are required to control several hundred miles of CTC equipment. Additional wires may be added to carry power for charging batteries.

Regular block signal track circuits

Insulated joints in rails

Telephone door

Maintainer's call light

Power switch machine enables dispatcher to throw switch automatically

Buried track circuit and control cables from relays and batteries

OS track circuit extends between signals at each end of switch; it operates the recording pen on the dispatcher's automatic train graph

A green aspect on this signal directs a train to leave the station track. When this signal is lined with a route, as indicated by a green or yellow aspect, the opposing signal will be red over red.

Insulated joints in rails

Dwarf signal has similar aspects but applies to a train standing on the side track

Passing track circuit

Main station track circuit

15

routes through the turnouts or infrastructure.

Let's look first at a simple interlocking case, one with just one turnout. These are very common across railroading, such as at the end of a controlled passing siding. For each interlocking plant, the entire interlocking is electrically one detected section, **15**. The detected section should include each turnout in the interlocking and all track from each of

the routes into the interlocking.

While each entrance would be another detected section outside the home signals, one detected section each for the single track approach, and each track leaving the turnout, the interlocking plant itself is a single detected section. Feeders to the track inside the interlocking, including switch points, lead rails, stock rails, frog, and all other rails up to the signals will be fed as described

above—from one power bus passing through a detection board (or channel, if your detector boards allow multiple channels).

Remember: in this example ALL feeders supplying power to any of the hot rails throughout the entire area between home signals must come from a bus wire that passes through the detector. Provided your rolling stock is properly equipped with resistive wheelsets on both ends, the equipment will draw a minute amount of current through the feeder for the detected section and therefore through the detector and the interlocking detected section will show occupancy until all equipment is clear of all rails within the interlocking. Logically this guarantees safety—once equipment is beyond the home signals, it cannot be fouling the turnout or the other routes.

Next, let's look at a double-track interlocking with "universal" crossovers. Universal in rail operations means that a train moving in any direction on any track can get to any other track within the interlocking. This arrangement, too, is very common throughout railroading worldwide.

In this example, we have home signals at four locations—one each at the entrance to the interlocking, in both directions, on both tracks. Between those signals, we have the two main tracks, as well as a left-hand and right-hand crossover arrangement between both tracks. Each track will need to be its own detected section, **16**.

Here we see a challenge—if each track in this universal interlocking has a separate bus wire and if each track needs to be independent of the other for detection, how do we deal with the crossovers themselves—i.e., how do we keep each turnout in the crossover isolated from its counterpart?

The answer is that we need to install isolated joints on each of the four rails of the crossovers between each main track. By wiring each of the diverging routes into the adjacent track bus wire, and by being careful to ensure that feeders to either side of the joint attach only to the proper bus, we can power all parts of the crossover, but have that power be drawn exclusively from the proper track bus.

One of the most challenging installations is that of an interlocking with "parallel routes"—that is, two routes through the turnouts side-by-side. For this to work, as in the diagram of Onondaga Cutoff interlocking CP 280, **17**, detected sections within the interlocking limits must be arranged so as to allow for a train on one route to not trigger detection on the other route. Each

Layout Command Control and signals

Layout Command Control, or LCC, is a free and open set of standards for layout control adopted by the National Model Railroad Association (NMRA) beginning in 2015. Intended to foster innovation and interoperability between manufacturers in the same way the NMRA DCC standard has, it also places a large amount of the detailed technical facets "under the hood" so the user can deal with more human-friendly function names. Layout Command Control is designed to run in parallel with DCC: each system has a separate bus, which allows control of accessories such as signals to be controlled without using the DCC command station.

A computer is used to help set up LCC devices, but unlike most controlled-signal systems, a computer is not required to run an LCC system as each device is self-sufficient and can operate on the "Many-to-Many" LCC architecture. ABS/APB signaling or grade crossings power up and become active as soon as the power is turned on to the LCC bus.

An exciting development is the Open LCC network supported by the NMRA. Its designers have had the opportunity to observe the issues and frailties of our older technologies and have designed a more robust system as a result. It also takes advantage of (and relies upon) the more powerful processors and chips that are available today at prices that we could only have dreamed of 20-30 years ago when other systems were developed and produced.

The RR Cir-Kits TowerLCC and SignalLCC modules work with BOD-8 block occupancy detector boards that have been around for a number of years. With the track detection block wired through the current sensing coil, placing an engine on the track will generate an LCC event and removing it will generate a second event. JMRI loads the configuration window, which resides in the LCC module, and using that window the user will assign the section's "human-readable" name, such as "425T" or "Mineola" using the "make sensor" function. One does not have to remember the LCC system event numbers once the sensor has been named. When you need to use those particular events when configuring any other device you look them up using the name you chose by using the "Search" function in the configuration window.

LCC is fully compatible with JMRI, but it does not require JMRI in order to operate. It is the first network that allows modelers to build a system that operates very much like the prototype with logic "in the field," meaning distributed around the layout—not just in a central computer that simulates the entire railroad. As signals and accessories grow more complicated and demand more data, and as layout owners start to provide more animation, LCC is positioned to provide the bandwidth to allow layouts to increase sophistication of accessories and animation to a new level.—*Dave Barraza*

route is separately detected so that the logic allows the routes to be independently operated.

Let's look at a parallel move. In this example of CP 280, train SEIN needs to enter the North Runner in Onondaga Yard in a westward direction from Track 1. This move is typical for many operations and is one of the moves for which the interlocking is designed. The dispatcher can line the turnouts for the no. 7 crossover and the no. 9 crossover, then pull up the signal for westward movement into the interlocking from Track 1.

Simultaneously, the crew for WAON-10, the road local, calls the Mohawk Dispatcher on the radio. He's all together, brake test complete, and ready to come down to CP-280 on the South Runner, looking to head east. Instead of having to wait for SEIN to finish its move, the Dispatcher can now line the no. 3 and no. 5 crossovers into reverse and pull up a signal for ON-10 to proceed eastward and cross from the South Runner to Track 1, then over to Track 2, all within CP 280 and while SEIN is slowly entering the yard from the east.

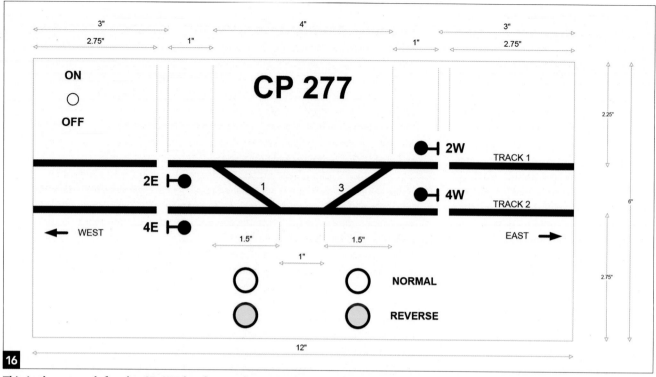

16

This is the artwork for the CP 277 local control panel, which controls a "universal" crossover.

The benefits here are obvious, especially when you consider that part of the issue is getting these trains out of the way of higher priority intermodal, autorack, or Amtrak train movements. If one had to wait for the other, capacity would suffer, which means more costs for the railroad and less-satisfied customers.

Parallel moves like this require thinking through the different moves you expect to make with your interlockings and building a detection system accordingly. In order to accommodate the full range of moves, we will see situations where a "normal" straight route through an interlocking

can contain multiple detected sections.

Take a normal move on Track 1 in the previous example. The no. 3 crossover and the no. 9 crossover both can be lined reverse, which creates the possibility of parallel moves. That means they each need detected sections on Track 1, so that the entire track isn't occupied at once. Therefore, insulated joints are placed between the turnouts of the no. 3 and the no. 9 turnouts on the straight route.

While I know how much work it is to get detection working, and while the concept of having all power moving through a single detector to each detected section isn't in itself

complicated, I also know how I learn: the hard way. Make no mistake: working detection is not a simple project. In any case it is easier to plan for detection circuits while you are laying and then wiring your track. It is more difficult to retrofit later. Therefore, it is good practice to include provisions for detection even if the signal system will be a longer time to bring to reality.

In summary, in building a reliable detection system, you are tackling the single most important piece of the signal system: the foundation. It is worth taking the time to do the intricate work to ensure that any and all power to each detected section flows through the detector, and to ensure that the detector is labeled and securely connected to the AIU. It is one of the seemingly invisible parts of the system, but it is the source of the logic for the larger system. From here, the rest begins!

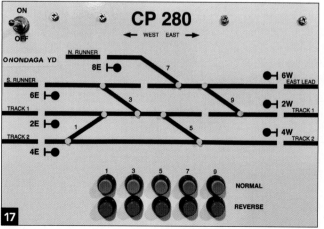

17

This is the signal layout for CP 280. Note at the right-hand side the parallel moves possible from the South Runner and East Lead to the main tracks below.

CHAPTER FIVE

Wiring signals for your model railroad

So, you are now able to run trains across your railroad like anyone else can—except your power is flowing to each block through a detector that can tell when power is being drawn and when it is not. On those blocks you have checked to make sure that the block detectors are working reliably. That is, for each occupied block, the detector shows occupancy and simultaneously no adjacent block is showing any current draw. You can walk with your train and watch each successive block detector trip to "on" beneath the railroad.

Freshly painted Santa Fe 3400 rolls westward through the intermediate signals between Summerfield and Black, Tex., on the Hereford Sub. The signals are by BLMA. *Sammy Carlile*

General Railway Signal type SA searchlight signal details east of Rochester, N.Y., in 2011. With detection in place, signals are next. *Nick Anshant*

Signals offer a modeler a chance to superdetail structures and add character to a layout. The details on these GRS type SA searchlights are apparent including the numberplate, which is considered part of the aspect and communicates to crews that these are automatic signals.

Conrail's network was assembled from a variety of predecessor railroads. Here at Neshanic, N.J., a former Lehigh Valley GRS searchlight signal functions as an automatic block signal (note the number plate) and displays "stop & proceed" following the daily passage of train Mail-3. *Jack Trabachino*

Let's stop for a minute here and consider your progress to date. Many modelers yearn for the chance to build a layout, and more so one that contains features they have always hoped to capture in model form. Not only do you have a layout under construction, you've laid track, wired your railroad, and now can sit back and run trains while watching that each and every separate block can tell when it is occupied. This in itself is a major accomplishment! You have arrived on the doorstep of the start of installing actual signal masts and hardware—this is a monument in itself and one worthy of a few minutes reflection, **1**.

This next leap for you will be determined by your end goal. If automatic signals are sufficient, and especially if you enjoy and are satisfied with the appearance of off-the-shelf signals, you have a few options at your disposal that can get your automatic signals up and running, **2**.

While wiring the signals themselves in the field is similar across all systems, the control is much more simple for those modeling automatic block signals (ABS) or using ABS in conjunction with a Timetable & Train Order operation. For these applications, there are several off-the-shelf systems to consider.

One of these is the system provided by Integrated Signal Systems; another is provided by RR-CirKits, and more are offered from Atlas Model Railroad Company, Azatrax, as well as Model Railroad Control Systems (MRCS), **3**.

If you are planning a full centralized system, including intermediate signals and full Centralized Traffic Control (CTC), while this chapter will discuss wiring signals to field hardware it will not go into the more complicated programming required for controlled signals. Discussion of those comes in the following chapters.

The best part? Your reliable block detection will be the basis upon which any system is built, **4**.

One of the simplest ways to have a working signal system is to install a system that is available as a series of boards and signals that work together with pre-programmed boards to simulate an automatic block signal system.

By definition, automatic block signal systems may or may not convey permission to use track—in fact, many timetable & train order operations used block signals in addition to the TT&TO as an extra layer of safety, not to authorize train movements. In a pure automatic system, there are no "controlled" signals—signals that allow a dispatcher to display a stop indication. Signals in an automatic block signal system only convey if the track ahead is clear or occupied, and show red signals too if there is a broken rail.

Rules varied from railroad to railroad. Lehigh & Hudson River, for example, had operators along the line but no remote controlled interlockings, 5. Each interlocking was manual with ABS between interlockings. Your railroad's rulebook for a certain stretch of track will need to be verified according to the prototype characteristics you are modeling, and if

continued on pg 84

4

Deep in a quiet West Virginia "holler," a pair of Norfolk & Western intermediate signals wait for the night's trains. Track 1, the farther track, is lined for an eastbound movement. The absolute-permissive signals show "clear" for an eastbound, with the westbound aspect at "stop & proceed," while Track 2 is not lined for movements and therefore in automatic mode shows "approach" in both directions.

5 **An excursion sponsored by High Iron Inc. using ex-Canadian Pacific 4-6-2 G5 no. 1286 splits the unique signal installation at Belvidere, N.J., on May 14, 1967. This is G Tower, where the Lehigh & Hudson River main line from Warwick, N.Y., joined the Penn Central (former PRR) Bel-Del main line. The westbound train is passing the position-light home signal for G, while the L&HR searchlight stands guard as part of the ABS system on the L&HR. This excursion was from Allentown, Pa., to Warwick and return. The locomotive was turned on the Warwick turntable.** *Rich Taylor*

6 This is a standard GRS type SA automatic signal installation near Oneida, N.Y., in 2011. *Nick Anshant*

7 The distant signal for CP Coeburn in Virginia in 2020 upgrades its aspect from "Stop & Proceed" (left, two red lights and a number plate) to "Restricting" as the dispatcher lines a route through the interlocking. *Jon Kayes*

8 In spots where signals must be located close to the aisle of the layout and in spots where manual uncoupling is regularly needed, it is prudent to install protection to ensure the fragile signal masts are not bumped. Ted Pamperin uses ¼" Plexiglas cut to shape.

Leaning heavily on its dynamic brakes, an eastbound coal train with a General Electric ES44AC on point exits tunnel no. 4 in Furnace Creek Canyon. Modern motive power and signalling are among many recent updates to Eric Brooman's ever-evolving HO scale Utah Belt. This automatic signal is displaying "stop." *Eric Brooman*

This is a GRS type SA automatic signal installation east of Rochester, N.Y., in 2011. Note the cabinet for electronics. *Nick Anshant*

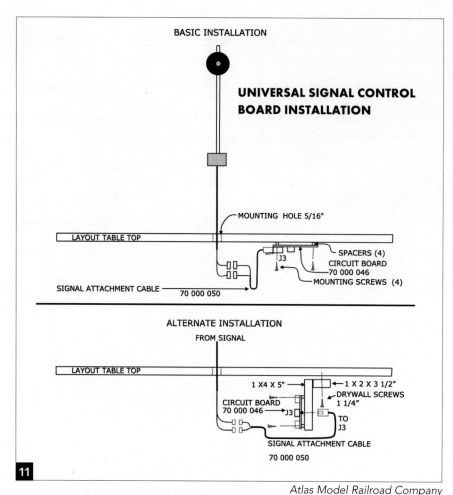

BASIC INSTALLATION

UNIVERSAL SIGNAL CONTROL BOARD INSTALLATION

MOUNTING HOLE 5/16"

LAYOUT TABLE TOP

SPACERS (4)
CIRCUIT BOARD
70 000 046
MOUNTING SCREWS (4)

J3

SIGNAL ATTACHMENT CABLE
70 000 050

ALTERNATE INSTALLATION
FROM SIGNAL

LAYOUT TABLE TOP

1 X 4 X 5"
1 X 2 X 3 1/2"
DRYWALL SCREWS
1 1/4"

CIRCUIT BOARD
70 000 046
J3
TO
J3

SIGNAL ATTACHMENT CABLE
70 000 050

11

Atlas Model Railroad Company

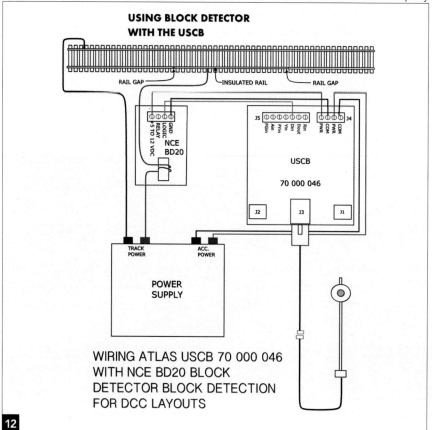

USING BLOCK DETECTOR WITH THE USCB

RAIL GAP — INSULATED RAIL — RAIL GAP

GND
LOGIC
RELAY
5 TO 12 VDC
NCE
BD20

J5
Rin
Rout
Din
Yin
Pin
Ain
RGin
COM
PWR
COM
PWR
J4

USCB

70 000 046

J2
J3
J1

TRACK
POWER
ACC.
POWER

POWER
SUPPLY

WIRING ATLAS USCB 70 000 046 WITH NCE BD20 BLOCK DETECTOR BLOCK DETECTION FOR DCC LAYOUTS

12

Atlas Model Railroad Company

continued from pg 81

you are freelancing then you can select one of those systems or design your own. Still, from a modeling standpoint, simple automatic block signal systems are available off the shelf and can be installed without much, if any, programming, **6**.

Because the system requires no formal control by dispatchers or operators, it also needs no interlockings at junctions or locations. This will limit the operations to a degree as there is no communication between the automatic signals and turnouts. That said, the system, like the prototype, will have aspects that change depending on the status of the block detection system, **7**.

Given the relative simplicity of the installation, and the cheaper cost, many prototype railroads had automatic block signals before upgrading to full Centralized Traffic Control (CTC). The same can be true for your railroad—if you are excited to get up and running, and your operations plans are satisfied by automatic signals, we can get right into it. Note, however, if your eventual plan includes controlled signals, an upgrade from ABS to CTC may most likely require moving signals around turnouts, or adjusting signals already located adjacent to turnouts, due to the nature of interlockings and CTC, **8**.

To begin, let's look at some of the "off the shelf" systems available to you for working automatic block signals. Integrated Signal Systems based in Florida offers a system using NCE or DCC Specialties block detectors to build an ABS system. The block detectors in this case are linked with their output to the Signal Controller board. Each controller operates two signal heads, one in each direction, or two heads on a multi-headed mast. The system is bi-directional on single track.

Integrated Signal Systems' signals perform exactly like prototype ABS systems so that as blocks are occupied, the signal controller board will change the aspects to reflect how many clear blocks are ahead. Additional signal controller boards are needed each time a signal is installed. More specialized systems can also be modeled.

For example, the Absolute-Permissive signal system can be modeled with the addition of a single pole, single-throw switch that allows display of automatic block signals in one direction only, with opposing automatic signals on single track showing red ("stop and proceed at restricted speed"), **9**.

Connections are made using wire inserted into screw terminals on the different boards. No soldering of these wires is required. On-board LEDs reflect the aspects of the signals and allow troubleshooting of any wiring errors without having to look at the signals themselves. Integrated Signal Systems manufactures and sells two different signal controllers, one that is specifically for searchlight-style heads and one that is for all signals and includes provisions for PRR position light signals, **10**.

Another possibility is the Atlas Model Railroad Company "21st Century Signal System," which includes many of the same capabilities as the ISS system and also advertises some other features that are interesting. The Atlas system and its Universal Signal Control Board (USCB) can be operated as a standalone operation where one signal runs independently of other signals and displays aspects in a simple timed manner, **11**. However, the same board also allows for ABS Block Signaling by connecting a number of Signal Control Boards together in a daisy-chain fashion, with input from the block detection, enabling representation of a prototypical block signal system.

This is a system across some or all of your main track where the occupancy of the blocks ahead and behind your train determines the aspects displayed by the signals, **12**. The number of blocks is controlled by a simple jumper setting on each signal control board.

Using the Atlas no. 215 switch panel with the USCB is another option for those looking only for the appearance of a lineside signal who would like to manually change colors with a basic selector switch. While not an indicator of block detection, this

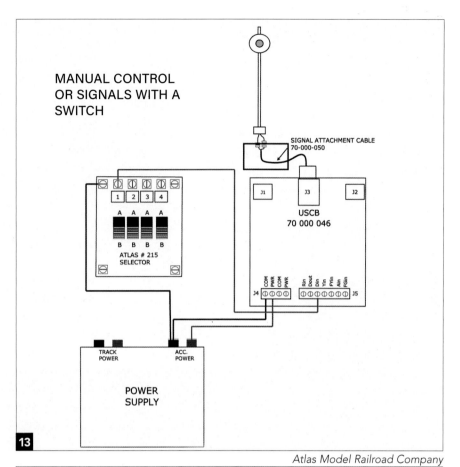

13

Atlas Model Railroad Company

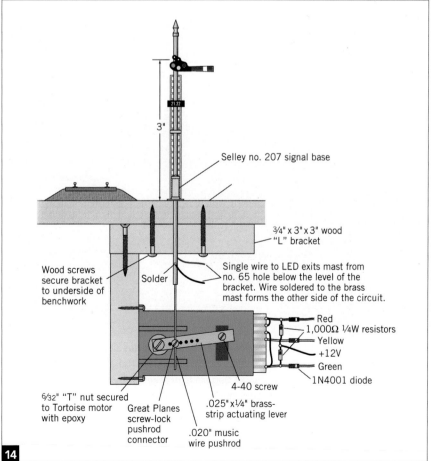

14

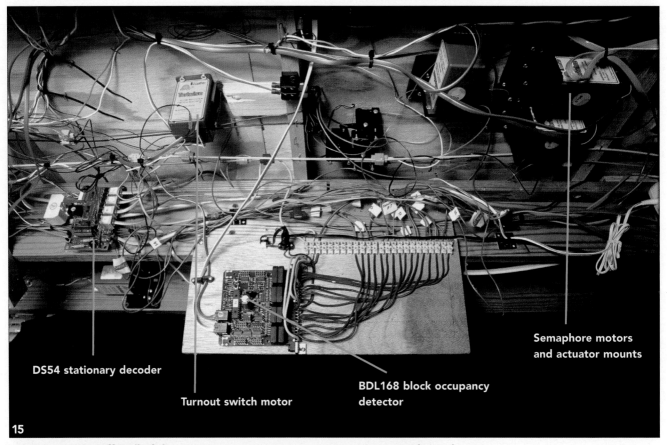

DS54 stationary decoder

Turnout switch motor

BDL168 block occupancy detector

Semaphore motors and actuator mounts

15

Many companies offer all of the components necessary to create an integrated signal system.

Rio Grande train No. 100 races eastward across Utah's desolate Green River Desert and passes into the interlocking at East Sagers, Utah, the morning of Oct. 2, 1987. The controlled siding at Sagers is protected by GRS Type D signals, which were common on the Rio Grande. *James Belmont.*

method is very useful for a train order or manual-block signal, **13**.

The new release of the Atlas system in 2018 has allowed additional features. These include a setting on the board to allow for simulating "Approach Lit" aspects, where the signal heads are dark until a train is nearby, as well as flashing aspects where certain signals are displayed as a flashing color instead of a solid color. On some railroads, in order to increase the number of indications available to train crews, such as intermediate restrictions, certain flashing aspects are used. These aspects are now supported with flashing yellow and green options and are automatically enabled for certain prototypes by a single jumper setting.

Many of the ABS installations across the country started as semaphore installations. Thankfully, resources exist on how to use semaphores instead of color-light or position-light signals, **14**.

While automatic signals are easier to set up using the off-the-shelf components, **15**, it is important to remember that by design ABS systems

16

Canadian Pacific AC4400CW 9781 leads oil loads under the unique modified signal bridge at CP 286 in East Syracuse, N.Y., in 2014. Railroads modified the original signal structures as needed when tracks were moved or as operational changes required. This bridge is the prototype for the bridge holding the eastward home signals at CP 280 on my Onondaga Cutoff.

Amtrak 276 meets Conrail TV-13 at CP 280 on the Onondaga Cutoff.

cannot display a stop indication, and therefore cannot support a true interlocking without additional effort. Adding controlled signals at those interlocking locations is entirely possible and we will look at that next, but it is another considerable layer of complication, **16**. If you're ready to take the plunge, let's turn the page!

CHAPTER SIX

The interlocking and your layout

Delaware & Hudson train 266 comes through CP 95 on J. Alex Lang's HO layout, which will represent the Allentown and Bethlehem area of Pennsylvania. Dwarf signals guard all staging tracks and a mast signal guards the main at the entry to the interlocking. Note the flat black patches painted on the layout surface under construction to help prevent glare. *J. Alex Lang*

The heart and soul of mainline railroading is the interlocking. By now in reading this book you have come across the term many times. Still, there is a lot of confusion on the difference between interlockings and junctions.

The bottom line here is that a junction is simply the intersection of two or more tracks, sometimes from two or more different railroads, sometimes different routes on the same railroad, sometimes a combination. These have existed from the earliest days of railroads. A junction may in some cases comprise only a single turnout. Larger junctions may be a series of turnouts, a diamond where two rail lines cross at grade, or any combination of those. From the first rail lines through to today, there are junctions all across the rail network.

An interlocking, by contrast, is a location on the railroad where turnouts and signals are integrated to control movement inside the interlocking plant, 1. The key defining characteristic of an interlocking, therefore, is that while tracks come together at that spot (just like a junction), an interlocking involves a series of mechanical or electrical devices that are linked in such a fashion so as to prevent conflicting movements on the same track.

So, interlockings often involve junctions, but not all junctions are interlockings. As we have seen in Chapter 1, this evolved over time, with the busiest junction locations being interlocked as need arose.

Other, non-junction interlockings are also used by railroads at most modern locations with a movable bridge on the main line. In some circumstances where operations require reversing trains, such as in commuter passenger operations, a controlled signal known as a "hold-out" signal capable of displaying "stop" (as opposed to the less restrictive "stop & proceed") is installed. Because of the controlled signals employed at that location, a hold-out signal is also technically an interlocking.

These last "controlled points" are most common on passenger train routes where some trains may be scheduled to stop and run in the opposite direction ("turned") at an intermediate location instead of the end of the line, and where yard movements may need "headroom" on the main track to move long cuts of cars. In both cases, the hold-out signals allow the limits of authority to be such to maximize operational flexibility.

Simple junctions may have signals—simple manual signs, for example, or a "stop sign" that sits on the lesser of the routes, commanding movements on that track to stop to check for clearance or ask for permission to cross. Your prototype likely has a document that describes these signals.

But these are not interlockings: with no mechanical or electrical connection between the signals and track hardware, the electrical and mechanical features present in an interlocking are not employed. This could be because the junction is lightly used or only handles certain trains at certain times of day, or because delays to the trains that do use the junction are acceptable given the nature of the traffic or the cost of upgrading the junction to include interlocking hardware. Without that interlocking hardware, a junction is not considered an interlocking.

For your railroad, let's begin applying these principles by looking at some layout considerations. If you already have your track in place, we will need to look at your track with an open mind. Some changes to the track may be necessary depending on your goals. If you're in the design phase, you're in luck; you are ahead of the curve and will be able to adjust your track plan to accommodate interlockings in a visually pleasing and operationally prototypical manner, 2.

For layout purposes, different sorts of interlockings are handled in the same manner. First, we examine the prototype and how railroads design and maintain interlockings.

Jeff Wilson's comprehensive article on building a mechanical interlocking is reprinted in the Appendix starting on page 126.

Nearly every single-track main line

A Baltimore & Ohio manifest freight is about to knock down the "clear" aspect on the home signal for Edison Interlocking and the diamonds with Bill Darnaby's Maumee Route. While two railroads cross at this interlocking, the B&O and Bill's Maumee Route, the interlocking machine works with both railroad's systems to protect all movements through the plant.
Bill Darnaby

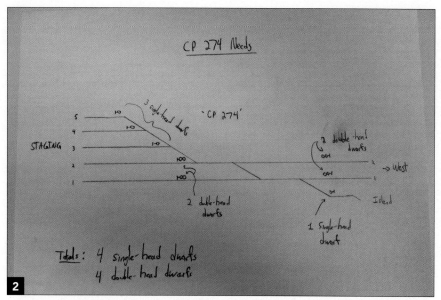

2

Early planning for signals and hardware can be a simple sketch. Early iterations of needs for CP 274 on my Onondaga Cutoff are shown here, with an overview of the system architecture for clarity. Sketches like these ensure common understanding and help avoid mistakes in construction.

around North America that has more than one train working on the route has a passing siding, **3**. The application of interlocking principles to the basic controlled passing siding is nearly universal and is a good start for our discussion on applying principles to your layout.

Here we have a photograph on the Montana Rail Link, the former Northern Pacific main line across Montana, **4**. This is the east end of the passing siding at Muir, Montana, the first siding on the east side of Bozeman Pass. This is mainline track and sees 8 to 12 trains daily; the train in the photograph is the SPOKCK (Spokane,

Wash., to Kansas City, Kan.).

The train is passing through the interlocking plant on its route east, having just passed a "clear" signal aspect on the silver-masted searchlight signals in the distance. Those signals mark the western boundary of the interlocking. The mast with the two heads showing red aspects marks the eastern boundary of the interlocking. As you can see, this is a one-switch interlocking and is part of the CTC-equipped MRL main line. The switch and routes are controlled by the dispatcher located in Missoula, using software on a computer server that drives the hardware in the field to display signal aspects.

What are some of the characteristics we need to consider to model this interlocking, or a similar one, on your layout? The answer is found in the design intent of this location: Muir is a passing siding, a location on the main line designed to allow two trains to pass one another.

This passing siding, like most on main lines across the continent, has an interlocking at each end that includes a switch between the main track and the siding. Trains either take the siding and wait for the passage of another train or they "hold the main" as is seen in the photograph. The dispatcher controls each of those switches accordingly to allow a train to enter the siding, and once the train is safely in the siding, the dispatcher will line the switch normal to allow another movement to pass on the main track.

Why only one switch? At Muir, there is no industrial track, no spurs to switch and no other main tracks crossing or diverging. The lesson here is that railroads only maintain what they need: your interlocking for a simple passing siding doesn't need extra switches.

Also, the location of this interlocking is important, both in relation to other sidings and in relation to the physical characteristics of the interlocking components. From an operational standpoint, this 2-mile-long controlled siding is approximately 8 miles from the next one to the east and about 11 miles from the next siding to the west. Optimal location would have the siding in the middle

3

Nickel Plate Road fast freight No. 49 behind class S-1 Berkshire 715 waits in the hole at Veedersburg, Ind., for late-running St. Louis-Cleveland passenger train No. 10. As soon as No. 10 clears the switch, the operator in the Peoria & Eastern tower lines the switch and the crossing for the westbound freight, giving it a red-over-green-over-red "medium clear" signal. This is automatic block (ABS) territory, so the center green signal also indicates that the next two blocks are clear. *Tony Koester*

4

Montana Rail Link train SPOKCK (BNSF overhead freight from Spokane, Wash., to Kansas City, Kan.) passes through the interlocking at East Muir, Mont.

of that distance, but a tunnel to the west of the siding is single track and therefore pushes the siding east. Thus the siding is as centrally located as is feasible in this case.

Keeping sidings evenly spaced increases operational efficiency by minimizing one train waiting for another coming from the opposite direction—both trains have similar distances to cover to reach the meeting point. The same principle applies on your railroad. If you have a single track main line, locate your sidings as evenly spaced as possible. On a multiple-track main line, locate your crossover interlockings as evenly as possible, **5**.

Signals are installed next to insulated joints in the track that define the boundaries of the detected section or interlocking, **6**. Note that for interlockings, the signals are always located just outside of the insulated joints, ensuring that equipment does not cross the boundary from a location where they can still see the signal. Put another way, signals are located so that if equipment stops short of a stop

signal, it is not inside the interlocking. The rules are strict about passing a stop signal, and penalties are severe. Crews usually stop with plenty of room to spare—better safe than sorry!

Track speed is also a factor in locating passing sidings. A slower route, with grades and restrictive curves, will include sidings spaced more closely together than a level, high-speed line across the open plains of the Midwest, for example. East Muir, like most prototype interlockings, is located on tangent track.

Note that this is a mountain railroad and that the curves are many. Still, the civil engineers and planners who laid out the route and the track chose one of the tangent spots for the interlocking. There is a reason for their consistency. First, switches with one leg straight and most moves on the straight leg minimizes maintenance of the switch.

But there is more. The tangent on either side of the interlocking allows for plenty of sight distance for crews

to observe signals before passing them, **7**. Trains are heavy and long and they take time to slow down or speed up. Crews need adequate time and distance to make it happen. While our model trains can change speed much more quickly than the prototype, our crews still need to be able to see the aspect ahead of time.

Like many aspects of model railroading, this is one that may require some creative thinking and adaptation on your railroad. The prototype usually has far more space available for their installations than we do! But the principle remains important—anyone running a train on your layout needs to be able to see the signal aspect before passing an automatic signal, and before entering the interlocking so as to determine how to handle the train.

On layouts, there are numerous examples of how modelers deal with the issue of signal visibility, **8**. Including all the features we need to operate the railroad prototypically means that some of the key locations would be pushed to less-than-optimal spots.

Establishing signal locations in the field, considering visibility, clearance, and clarity

Signals cannot be complied with by crews without clear visibility by approaching trains. They should be located on tangent track or, if they must be on curved track, they must be constructed in a way that crews can see their aspect with enough time to react. Signals that govern entry and routes into and through interlockings do more than just mark the entry: they define a hard location where the rules of train movement change and provide a physical marker for crews performing work. Their location is critical.

One key is to make sure that you check clearances as you install signals. If signals cannot be seen due to layout constraints, consider "repeater" signals displayed in the fascia. On the Onondaga Cutoff, eastbound signals at CP 282 face a backdrop; therefore the aspects are displayed on signals mounted above the drop-in ceiling and visible to crews through a window in the ceiling.

Second, all turnouts within an interlocking MUST be FULLY located between the signals. There are rare exceptions in extremely complicated interlockings such as those in New York Penn Station in New York City; however, signals must be placed so that equipment can stop short of the signal and be completely clear of the switch points and any other track in the limits of the interlocking.

Third, signals must be placed far enough along the track so that equipment on one track is completely clear of equipment occupying an adjacent track. In other words, if a locomotive is on a track, waiting at a "stop signal" indication, the signal must be located so that there is no way any part of the locomotive is fouling the adjacent route.

Fourth, signal location should be selected to ensure crews operating equipment understand where they are and what tracks the signals govern. On North American railroads, with the engineer sitting on the right-hand side of the cab looking forward, this means almost all signals are mounted on the right side of the track.

Finally, don't forget the basics—the signal itself must be far enough from the centerline of track to avoid contacting on-track equipment. This sounds obvious, but you need to measure carefully on curves and diverging routes and double-check yourself by running your longest piece of equipment past the proposed location. In some cases, the only reasonable way to achieve this is to use special signal types to avoid the clearance envelope, such as signal bridges, cantilever or bracket masts, or dwarf signals.

Sometimes signal aspects require creative solutions. On the Onondaga Cutoff, the CP 282 eastward home signals face the backdrop. Mirrors would be confusing and detract from the finished scene. So, Dave mounted "repeater" signals into the ceiling, allowing operators to see their aspect while keeping the integrity of the scene and layout fascia.

A closer view of the signal "window" for the eastward aspects at CP 282.

CP 277 before scenery, displaying its first "clear" aspect in 2013. Compare this view to the image on page 5—the Onondaga Cutoff has come a long way in 7 years!

In some cases, dwarf signals are used for main line home signals, such as those shown here for CP 285 in East Syracuse N.Y. Track 2 is lined for a westbound with an approach-medium aspect, an advance warning that the next signal is showing medium clear for a diverging move. Advance aspects and logical sequencing allows crews to adjust their speed accordingly.

On the Onondaga Cutoff, CP 282 is such a spot. CP 282 is at the west end of Onondaga Yard and includes the junction between the Minoa & Euclid line and the Conrail Chicago Line. As such, it is a busy universal interlocking with seven different home signals. To maximize the length of Onondaga Yard, CP 282 had to be pushed around a curve and up against a backdrop.

This meant that the eastward home signals on the main line, mounted on a signal bridge, would face the backdrop and be impossible to see from the aisle. The signal bridge and eastward home signals are at the entrance to the interlocking, which is where they should be. The problem is their aspects are displayed facing away from the aisle where an operator is standing—the entrance to the interlocking is located at the pass-through into the backdrop where the railroad heads west downgrade.

We looked at adding signals to the fascia or mounting signals backward or angled on the signal bridge. We even looked at adding a mirror so that crews could see their aspects reflected back at them. Visually, however, each of those ideas had serious drawbacks.

The aspects needed to be displayed in a logical manner, so that crews could tell which signal was theirs on a two-track line, **9**. For an operating layout with double track, it was important to have crews remember where to look for their aspects.

Mirrors made it confusing, especially at night, since it appeared to be an aspect in the opposite direction. Signals in the fascia did not stand out as much as we hoped, especially when located next to the local control panel and its turnout-position indicator lights.

Perhaps the worst part was that the constraints of the layout had crew members on the other side of the backdrop, following their train working up the hill from the staging yard at CP 294. How could I have these signals visible from both sides of the backdrop?

The solution we implemented was above us: by mounting repeater

5

Utah Railway SD40 9005 leads an 81-car export coal train through Gilluly, Utah, past GRS Type D signals protecting the interlocking at the crossover in the double-track main line shared with Denver & Rio Grande Western in 1995. *James Belmont*

6

We can learn a lot from the prototype. Here we see insulated joints at CP-BOYD on the Raritan Valley Line of NJ Transit. Note how the joints are located: staggered, to reduce impact loads from passing axles to one side at a time, and parallel to or beyond the signal mast in the background.

signals on top of the wall supporting the backdrop, and cutting a "window" into the drop-in ceiling tiles below those repeaters on each side of the backdrop, now crews could simply look up as their train climbed the grade and see their aspect long before the train arrived at the interlocking limits. While this is an unconventional solution, it is the best for its designed use and allows the interlocking on

the railroad to remain in a space that optimizes other parts of the operation.

Even with that adaptation, the westward home signals at CP 282 and the westward home signals at CP 280 farther east required their own adaptations to achieve the best viewing angles for operators. At the big signal bridge that marks the east end of CP 282 and supports the westward home signals, the railroad makes a sweeping

7

Dwarf signals were as varied as standard signals, and the Baltimore & Ohio was no exception. Here a classic B&O color position light dwarf signal stands on tangent track guarding diamonds with Conrail outside Gary, Ind., in 1998. *Jack Trabachino*

8

J. Alex Lang used mirrors to allow crews in the aisle to see signal aspects leaving staging. This way the signals face the correct direction and the mirror allows aspect visibility while minimizing confusion. In difficult situations, modelers must adapt. *J. Alex Lang*

9

The westbound signal on the right shows green-over-red—"clear"—on a foggy April 1973 morning on the Chesapeake & Ohio in Quinnimont, W.Va. The rectangular tower (QN Cabin in C&O parlance) atop the yardmaster's office was closed when CTC was installed. The C&O made extensive use of cantilever signal bridges. *Tony Koester*

10

CSX train Q-119 moves international stacks west, passing the unique former New York Central bracket-mast home signal at CP 293 in Syracuse, N.Y., in 2014. New York Susquehanna & Western interchanges with CSX here, and its SY-1 job waits to the right at a stop signal for the stack train to clear.

turn around the end of Onondaga Yard. This meant that the bridge would be mounted above curved tracks below, and that the signals on the bridge would need to be viewed from a different angle.

On the prototype, where signals are located in a curve, the heads will be adjusted to point down the railroad toward the first point where the crews can view the aspect. We followed suit on the signals mounted on that bridge—each is turned about 20

degrees to the left of center, enough so the heads point to a spot farther down the track than the start of the curve.

Another unique adaptation on the prototype was mounting the signals for one track higher than the other, so that trains on the outside of a two-track curve could see their aspects even if a train were on the adjacent track. New York Central, and later Penn Central and Conrail, used this technique on the interesting bracket-mast signal installation on the prototype at CP SJ

(Syracuse Junction), later called CP 293 in Syracuse and Solvay, NY, **10**.

Inspired by this example at Syracuse, the westward bracket mast on the Onondaga Cutoff at CP 280 was planned and constructed with a similar design. The signals governing Track 2 are mounted higher than those on Track 1, allowing for the proper sight distance even if a train on Track 1 limits the views possible for crews on Track 2.

One constant across different

11

Common details at interlockings are easy to include thanks to parts available from Details West, Details Associates, Atlas, BLMA and others. Electrical cabinets and switch machines add to the detail at CP 280 on the Onondaga Cutoff.

interlockings in North America is that each is marked on all boundaries by home signals. Home signals, as you will recall, are controlled by the dispatcher or operator and govern the entrance to and movement through the interlocking limits. Therefore, the first step in creating interlockings is to establish locations for home signals that complies with the basic requirements of any such signal.

If you did this while reading Chapter 4, you have already worked through the challenges here, but it bears repeating. Home signals must be located at points clear of all moving parts of the turnouts so that a train stopped at the signal is clear of all other tracks or equipment on all other parts of the interlocking. Home signals must be visible to operators of equipment approaching the interlocking.

Details

Like any good model, details make a world of difference. Interlockings are loaded with details for the modeler to consider, **11**. While signals are part of every interlocking, your era will determine a great deal of the details you can include, **12**. Early

12

Here are General Railway Signal Co. searchlight details at Toston, Mont.

interlockings, with their mechanical systems, included long runs of rods connected to levers to move switch points and semaphore arms. All of these can be modeled and add a superdetailed look to any interlocking.

Early interlockings also included a tower, which was the control center for the interlocking and the office for the operator. Towers were iconic and

usually built according to standard plans by the railroad to house the interlocking machine and hardware. Different railroads had different and distinct architecture.

In some cases one can tell what company owned the railroad by looking at the towers along the route. Towers for your layout may be available as kits from different suppliers, and

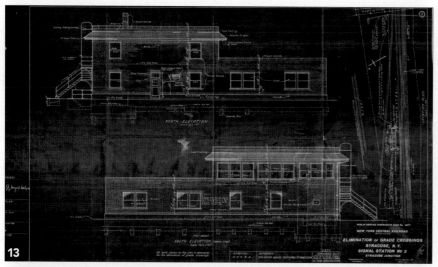

13

A blueprint sheet shows the plans for reconstruction of the GRS signal tower at Syracuse Junction, Syracuse, N.Y.

14

Details West switch machines simulate the look of the prototype machines nicely as seen here at CP 282 on the Onondaga Cutoff.

15

Signal bungalows are important details for modern interlockings. Many interlockings today have the station name on a sign attached to the bungalow, or stenciled on the bungalow directly. Conrail TV-14 speeds past.

16

Chesapeake & Ohio Mikado no. 1111 holds the controlled siding at Allegheny while a mail train flies by on the main. Ted Pamperin has included electrical cabinets and battery boxes along with power and communications lines on poles, adding to the scene.

plans for others can be found online or perhaps through the historical society for your prototype, **13**.

As interlockings were upgraded to electric or pneumatic switch machines, the levers disappeared, replaced by cables. In some cases the cables were pole-mounted and in others they were buried, but in every case the switch machine became a fixture next to the points on the switch, **14**.

Another part of signal installations are the various signal cases and bungalows to allow for interlocking construction and maintenance. These cases are generally located near the signals, **15**. Many interlockings also have a battery backup in case of commercial power failure; you can also include these in your modeling. Appropriate detail parts like switch machines, signal cases, and bungalows are made by Details West and Detail Associates, **16**.

Protecting those same details is also important: for delicate items close to the edge of the layout, your scale signals and details need protection from passing elbows and bodies during layout work or operating sessions, **17**. It's a crushing feeling when so much work goes into something scale, only to see it damaged or destroyed in a full-size accident!

17

A 1/8"-thick sheet of Plexiglas is a barrier to damage from elbows at CP 280.

Wiring interlockings—overview

Each interlocking will be controlled through a series of computer boards. While the boards differ depending on which system you choose, the idea is the same insofar that the turnouts and signals will all be routed through the boards which are controlled by logic built into the software installed on the boards and in your PC, **18**.

As can be seen at right, there are several components in the chain of command. Block detection from the NCE BD-20 boards comes in through the NCE AIU boards via the NCE command bus. Communication between the NCE command station and the PC is directly through the NCE-USB connection, where JMRI can "talk" to NCE. From the PC running JMRI, components are arranged to allow the PC to talk to the Digitrax SE8c signal decoders via a LocoNet command bus system.

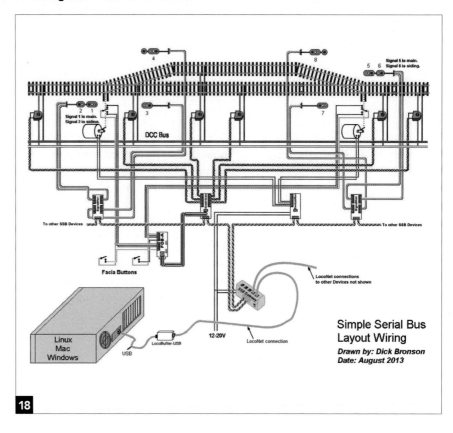

18

Signal 1 is main.
Signal 2 is siding.

Signal 5 is main.
Signal 6 is siding.

DCC Bus

To other SSB Devices

To other SSB Devices

Facia Buttons

LocoNet connections
to other Devices not shown

Linux
Mac
Windows

LocoBuffer-USB

USB

12-20V

LocoNet connection

Simple Serial Bus Layout Wiring

Drawn by: Dick Bronson
Date: August 2013

19

A classic Baltimore & Ohio bracket
mast signal stands on the CSX
Philadelphia Subdivision in 2011.
Nick Anshant

Instead of a Digitrax command station, we use a Digitrax UP5 on the OC for power and the Locobuffer-USB by RRCirkits.com as the interface between the PC and LocoNet. Each of the SE8c signal decoders is linked on the LocoNet. From the SE8c, each Tortoise switch machine has two power leads to line the machine. Also from the SE8c, 10-wire ribbon cable runs from each signal driver socket out to the location of the signals themselves where it is attached to a Digitrax Terminal Strip Mounting Kit (TSMK). The TSMK contains screw terminals for each of the wires to the signals themselves—no need for soldering under the layout. All this necessarily means quite a bit of wire beyond the track power and block detection we focused on in Chapter 3, **19**.

LocoNet & wiring signals

The specifics of controlled signals are covered in Chapter 7. However, a general overview is of use to the reader to provide a framework for your interlockings, and will help

you understand the basics so we can physically install signals on your railroad before programming them.

For the Onondaga Cutoff, we located SE8c boards in four different locations around the layout, roughly equidistant from interlockings that would be controlled by the board. For proper control, each switch machine will rely on a unique identifier which is assigned based on the Digitrax protocol.

The SE8c manual has specific instructions on how to ensure we accomplish that. We began by connecting each Tortoise switch machine to the SE8c, following instructions included with the hardware. Each SE8c requires the board to be identified to the PC. Following the instructions from Digitrax and keeping a close record of each address will help ensure success.

Each board then will have a unique name, and each switch machine will also then be uniquely identified by the SE8c and the PC. Again, keep a strict list of the name of each machine for use once we begin programming in Chapter 7.

In designing the Onondaga Cutoff, we used a LocoNet set up to power and communicate with the switches and signals for the system. The "brain" behind the aspects the signals display is the signal decoder, a circuit board connected to JMRI via LocoNet that drives the aspects themselves.

For the Onondaga Cutoff, the board is the Digitrax SE8c signal decoder, which includes enough output to drive 32 signal heads and up to 8 pairs of Tortoise machines. Other signal decoders and manufacturers exist and many have attractive features.

Here are a few features to consider: the number of heads and switch machines a decoder can control, whether your signals are 3-color LED, 2-color LED, common cathode or common anode wiring, position lights, color position light, etc.; and whether the boards support flashing or approach-lit aspects, and whether or not you can include a local control panel or button to allow for field control of an interlocking.

Local control was a major issue for the Onondaga Cutoff, **20**. Seeing as how a full-scale operating session only happens about one time a month, I needed a simple way to throw switches during construction, cleaning, or leisurely running trains between sessions, **21** and **2** in Chapter 3.

The SE8c included the terminals to attach a momentary-on pushbutton that in turn would line the turnout. I took it a step further and mounted the pushbuttons in a replica panel designed and professionally printed on aluminum sheet to replicate the prototype located in the bungalow at every interlocking, **22**.

To run the SE8c, follow the instruction manuals provided. To run a LocoNet system in addition to an NCE or other control system, we need to take a few extra steps. LocoNet for signaling does NOT require a Digitrax command station. The commands will be issued by the computer, translated by the LocoBuffer USB and understood by the SE8c.

From the COM port on the PC, connect the Locobuffer USB per its directions and then connect the other side of the Locobuffer USB to a Digitrax UP5 board. UP5 boards are the "plug in" stations for Digitrax and include a power supply via a "wall wart" plug. One side of the UP5 is then wired to the Locobuffer USB, and the other to the first SE8c, which in turn is wired to the next SE8c and so on using the Digitrax command bus flat cables.

Our preference on the Onondaga Cutoff was to install an SE8c at different areas around the layout, close to as many switches and signals as possible. While this increased the necessary length of the flat-cable runs, it minimizes the length of the ribbon cable and wiring at the interlockings and was a worthwhile trade off.

The Digitrax system is built to work seamlessly with itself, with each SE8c being wired using 10-wire ribbon cable to the Digitrax TSMK boards, small computer boards that are the interface between LocoNet and the signals themselves, **23**. The instructions are clear, but it is worth noting here that

20

It is helpful to begin operations as soon as possible. Long before scenery and working signals, Dave used leftover Masonite from his backdrop installation to create temporary local control panels, with double-pole, double-throw toggles to control Tortoise switch machines wired in series with light-emitting diodes for indicators. These stood in for more than a year while he and his operators finalized interlocking planning and design.

the SE8c comes with a test mast on Driver 1 that will include a "signal"—a simple PC board with LEDs soldered in place to represent a two-head signal on the railroad.

Upon powering the SE8c, the test board will light both red LEDs—the red is "hot" on the SE8c from start up. Once you follow the test procedures in the manual, the powered red terminal allows you to run your ribbon cables and to install your actual layout signals one by one. Your cables will mimic the test setup, but will run to each TSMK in order to light your signals, **24**.

Each TSMK has two terminals, one each for one head of a signal. For signals with three heads, you will use two TSMKs—JMRI allows any TSMK to drive any head, so the aspects do not depend on using the same TSMK or two adjacent TSMKs. Follow the instructions on the SE8c carefully here.

Digitrax makes the ribbon cables, but you can also make your own from a roll of the ribbon cable in bulk. Cut the lengths you need and create ends using one of the kits available from

21

Installation of the fascia is done concurrently with the installation of the final local control panels. Like the prototype, each interlocking can be cut in separately, a more reasonable way to troubleshoot issues and ensure success.

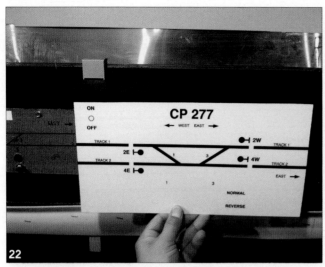

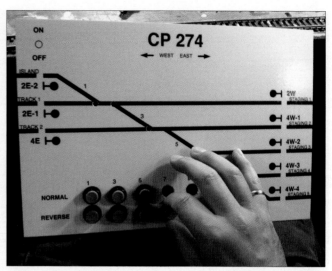

Dave tested the fit of the new permanent local control panel for CP 277, next to the temporary panel added to support operation as soon as possible.

This is the large panel for CP 274 on the Onondaga Cutoff during the installation of the pushbutton controls.

This is typical SE8C wiring. There are three of these panels that control the signals, detection, and turnout pushbuttons to help move traffic on Sammy Carlile's Hereford Sub. This view also shows the Circuitron rolling stock detector. All components were mounted on small pieces of white painted plywood, wired and tested at the work bench before installation. *Sammy Carlile*

electronics supply houses, being careful to replicate the alignment of the pins on the Digitrax test cable that comes with your SE8c. For your first try at lighting your signals, it is helpful to do one at the computer before starting at a field spot on the layout to get a feel for the connections and to easily check the aspects as you proceed, **25**.

Like the SE8c, use the directions fastidiously for the TSMK. You will note that on the TSMK each port is labeled for red, yellow, green, aux, and common. Your signals will be wired

into each port as appropriate for the color, which can be tested by hooking up the common wire and then testing each of the other wires to the red port.

Again, keep in mind that the red port is by default hot with the Digitrax system. If the signal's green light comes on, that wire should be permanently fastened to the green terminal, yellow to yellow, and then finally red to red. The Aux terminal is needed if a user decides to use the Digitrax system for position lights or to include accessories on some railroad's signals such as lunar

white lamps (B&O, D&RGW, etc). The Aux terminal can be left unused for color-light signals.

With this first test completed, it is time now to finally "plant" signals on your layout, drilling holes so as to thread the connecting wires for the signal through the hole before mounting the signal. This is intricate and fine work; take your time.

Once the wires are all pulled through the layout surface and the signal is sitting where it will be fixed in place, mount the TSMK within a short distance to your signal, and then run the ribbon cable from the SE8c all the way to the TSMK in accordance with the directions. Wiring signals with the Digitrax system is also covered extensively through the SE8c manual, with an example much like my sample interlocking at East Muir.

This installation too is tested according to the Digitrax instructions before proceeding further. In some cases, the common wires can be twisted together on each TSMK and installed in just one of the common terminals. Resistors built into the TSMK boards protect the sensitive LED circuits to help ensure no damage to signals as you work through your testing.

Start with Driver1. Run the ribbon cable from Driver1 to the TSMK below the signal installation. As you attach each of the signal leads to the TSMK, attach the common wire, and

24

Typical wiring for a Digitrax SE8c signal decoder is shown here. The colorful ribbon cables run from one of eight nodes out to the Digitrax TSMKs, which allow for interface between the ribbon cables from the decoder and the leads from the signal heads. *J. Alex Lang*

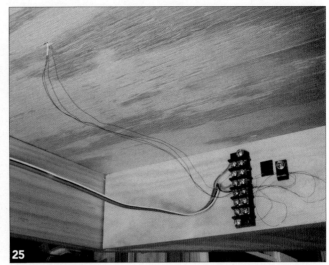

25

Alex used a simple terminal strip as the interface between the ribbon cable and signal leads in this case. This approach requires appropriate resistors in line with the signal leads to protect the bulbs or LEDs from too much current draw. *J. Alex Lang*

then touch each power lead to the red terminal. If red lights up, temporarily set that aside and test the yellow and green colors by touching them to the red terminal. After determining that they work, attach each color to the appropriate terminal on the TSMK, including the red. Your signal head should now show red.

Again, keep close record on a list of which board and which driver on the board relates to each signal head. This will be central later as we program the signal aspects on the PC. At this point, repeat for each head—and after some work you will have an interlocking that looks a lot like the prototype on a quiet day, with red signals signifying "stop signal" in all directions. Now is a good time to take a break and run some trains—to test your system! Look for clearance, check viewing angles, and take a minute to enjoy, **26**. We are now very close to our goal of controlled signal operation—and Chapter 7 holds the final keys to move forward, **27**.

26

Conrail train Mail-3 curves out of staging on J. Alex Lang's layout. Alex installed signals on the bottom deck and is wisely running trains on that deck first to ensure smooth operations before construction of the upper decks. *J. Alex Lang*

27

Home signals shine red in the dusk at CP 286 in East Syracuse, N.Y.

CHAPTER SEVEN

Controlled signals for your model railroad

Maumee local No. 20 crosses the Chesapeake & Ohio diamonds in the interlocking at Gastonia, Ohio, on Bill Darnaby's layout. The CTC machine at right controls the interlocking and is used by the operator to move trains through the plant. The red lights on the board are the track occupancy lights showing the presence of the Maumee train. *Bill Darnaby*

As we have seen in the prototype history, railroads first developed mechanical signal logic to control interlocking plants with large levers interlocked with physical pins and moved by brute force. With the development of electrical devices in the late 1800s, mechanical logic was replaced with electromechanical installations with large banks of relays.

Both systems were arranged so as to provide single-path logic protection against conflicting moves and to protect following moves from coming too close to the equipment ahead of them. Today, dispatchers and operators use either a physical CTC machine or a computer screen to interact with the system and to establish and line routes, **1**.

With the technology and systems available today in the hobby, we can accomplish much the same thing on our model railroads in much the same way. Prototype CTC machines require extensive wiring and power to each and every component—such a system requires an intimate knowledge of mechanical and electromechanical relays needed for it to function. There is a reason prototype railroads have entire departments of engineers and technicians to build and maintain their signal systems.

We touched on the idea of mechanical interlockings and their controlled signals in Chapter 6, **2**. These "islands" of control allow controlled signals for your railroad, but in the style of the old trunk line railroads: manual coordination from tower to tower along the route, which requires staffing the interlockings as well as a block line for tower operators to communicate with each other, **3**.

The remainder of this book will be dedicated to helping us add the final layer to signalized railroading—centralized dispatching, replicating the CTC used by all today's major railroads.

As computing has grown and as its use in model railroad signaling has developed, several systems are now available to prototypically model the operation of the electromechanical system by using only solid-state hardware and basic programming. This is to say that by connecting a computer to the layout and building a computer-driven system, a layout owner can have a CTC board that controls signals on the layout without all the moving parts and hard-wiring needed for a machine driven by relays. We can build an installation with traditional appearance and user interface, but with all the background logic running on hardware

1 CSX piggyback train Q009 rolls west toward the approach medium aspect displayed for movement through CP 433 in Buffalo, N.Y. This signal aspect communicates to the crew that the next signal will be for a crossover move.

2 One of Susquehanna's distinctive Russian Decapods heading a westbound extra freight gets a clear signal at Sparta Junction and its interlocking. Each of the four signals here, three mast-mounted signals and a lone dwarf, is a home signal. These mark the entrance to the interlocking.

and software available to modelers, **4**.

For even more modern applications, there is an even simpler way to accomplish true CTC control. As we have discussed, most Class 1 railroads moved from electromechanical CTC machines in the 1970s, 1980s and 1990s to solid-state dispatching systems directly from a computer with a monitor. Systems like C/MRI and JMRI both allow a layout to be attached to and controlled using the

computer and an overlay to the JMRI system—"Computer Automated Traffic System" (CATS)—allows for a Windows-based approach to dispatching your layout using the computer via a straight-line diagram on the computer monitor similar to modern dispatching systems across North America, **5**.

Whether you choose computer control with a CTC machine interface or a computer monitor interface, the

3

A Pennsylvania RR manifest is about to cross the diamonds with the Maumee main line at Sciotovale, Ohio.

4

Big Chesapeake & Ohio 2-6-6-6 Allegheny no. 1610, having pushed another loaded coal drag to the summit, is now awaiting its chance to turn on the big turntable at the summit. The operator at A Tower has lined the route, and pulled up the signal aspect.

benefits of using such a system for your dispatching are many. First, modern components are readily available and are adjustable using some basic computer programming. Second, their functionality can be made identical to the older system of a dispatcher and tower crews in the field, which suggests an authentic system to operators on your layout. Third, the modern solid-state components generate far less heat than the old electromechanical systems

and require far less space than is required by banks of relays, transistors and power supplies.

Computer systems like Bruce Chubb's C/MRI and the open-sourced JMRI have allowed more people access to the logic required to make the system work, **6**. Both include a basic Microsoft Windows-style format that allows for creating a line diagram in the software. Each line can be labeled and linked to the specific block it

represents, and once entered you have a computer model of your layout.

Phil Monat uses a fully-functional replica CTC machine for dispatching his Delaware & Susquehanna Railroad. Like many layouts with a CTC machine, Phil selected the C/MRI system to drive the block detection, turnout control, and signal control. See "Just what is this C/MRI anyway?" on page 44.

Phil used the C/MRI block detection modules throughout his railroad, running to field nodes to collect the occupancy information. The machine is connected to the field nodes via a four-wire shielded pair. This is linked to software running on a personal computer (PC) for a fully digital system. Software running on the PC listens to inputs from the field nodes and block detectors and displays track occupancy based on that input.

Phil, who works with lighting professionally, built many of his own boards for the components of the system. These include input and output (I/O) boards, several detector boards, and switch machine driver boards. While some will choose to make their own components, the original C/MRI system is available from JLC

Enterprises Inc. at jlcenterprises.net

The Chubb system is widely used among signaled model railroads that operate. The components are accessible and universally programmable (using Microsoft Basic). Some of the more advanced functions including directional traffic locking, electric locks, time releases, etc., take some Basic code to execute and assistance is available from JLC or from various internet resources.

For his CTC machine, Phil purchased aluminum sheet and components and constructed it himself. It is a beautiful part of his layout and one that very much captures the feel of the prototype. Phil designed the layout of the board ahead of time and had the aluminum silk-screened for painted graphics, lettering, and labels. The machine is permanently mounted on a wooden desk assembled to support it. Phil stained the wood to represent photos of old CTC offices and finished it with polyurethane finishes.

The machine holds one node, which accounts for 256 inputs and outputs in C/MRI. The lights are LEDs purchased thru electronic supply houses as are all the components with the exception of the switch and signal toggle switches. Phil used Rix Products (rixproducts.com/product-category/ctc-knob/) parts for those elements.

CTC boards are appropriate for modeling CTC from its inception in the mid-1920s through about the late 1980s, by which time most mainline railroads were making the switch to solid-state electronics.

Solid-state electronics offer additional possibilities including a great resource in JMRI and CATS. On the Onondaga Cutoff, I began by connecting a PC to the internet and downloading the JMRI software. The JMRI website is open-sourced, free, user-friendly and has a tremendous amount of information available online.

Computer Automated Traffic System (CATS) is a piece of software originally written by Rodney Black to run as a file that refers to the "library" of JMRI itself. (Refer to the CATS manual.) I recommend downloading the latest stable version of JMRI and

The massive 2-6-6-6 steam engine gingerly approaches the turntable at restricted speed as dictated by signal indication.

installing it on your PC and I will guide you through that process shortly.

Looking back at Chapter 4, you wired each and every block into its own unique channel in an AIU, which itself is given its own command bus address. Each of these was labeled with a description. Our next job is to build a panel in JMRI that replicates the signaled track of your railroad. The easiest way to begin this is with ... paper and a pencil.

What? Paper and pencil? Well, yes: you need to create what railroads call a "line diagram" for your route, showing each signaled track, each turnout, and how they relate to each other.

Note that this will not be "to scale" as the most important parts (turnouts) outweigh the operational importance of other track where there are no switches, **7**.

As you can see here, now we have a schematic that at a glance looks like a modern day dispatcher screen, **8**. Now that we have the diagram, we can add in our blocks as installed on the railroad. I use a short vertical line to delineate the insulated joints.

JMRI is a wonderful package that includes the ability for you to create your own straight-line diagram in a software package called PanelPro. However, using our approach with

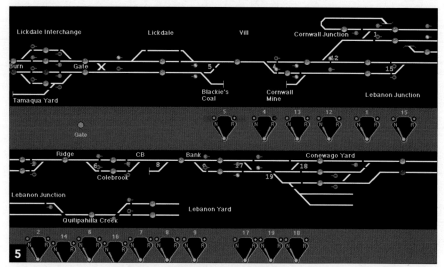

PanelPro, another JMRI software module, gives you the ability to design virtual CTC panels allowing you or your dispatcher to remotely control turnouts and signals all over your layout. *Diagram courtesy of Nick Kulp*

This is the C/MRI wiring and components for the signal system on Ted Pamperin's HO scale Chesapeake & Ohio layout. Bundled wiring, clear labeling, organized hardware and color-coded wire make for a neat, albeit complicated, installation.

CATS, we will use the CATS software to start with a blank canvas, so to speak.

Installing JMRI and CATS on your railroad

Our goal here is to guide you to the process of installing the software and making the connections to your railroad.

Start by visiting the web: JMRI. org is the website for the Java Model Railroad Interface and is the start of our journey towards controlled signals on your railroad, **9**.

From the homepage, read down and you will see the different download options. You're looking for the latest "stable" version of their software: the current production release. Since JMRI is always being updated by different programmers, the software is always changing, but the base model is stable. Check to make sure that the current version of the CATS software works with the version of JMRI you download. Click on the CURRENT PRODUCTION RELEASE link and it will take you to the download page.

Before we dig into CATS, let's get JMRI up and running. From the JMRI home page, download the JMRI software for your operating system (iOS, Windows, or Linux). Also, while you are on that screen, you can see a link for CATS, the Computer Automated Traffic System, as well. CATS will be a layer of software using the base of JMRI for us to build our interlockings on the computer, **10**.

Once the JMRI software is downloaded, the computer will ask you if you want to install. Click YES—you can install according to the default path on the computer. (For up-to-date step-by-step instructions on downloading and installing JMRI, reference the install guides listed on the left sidebar of the download page.)

Once JMRI is installed, you have the capability of having your PC talk directly to your layout command station and for your layout to communicate with the PC. Regardless of which system you have chosen for DCC, you can take the next few steps by following the instructions that JMRI uses to connect to the command stations. For example on the Onondaga Cutoff, to connect the NCE Power Pro 5-amp system to the computer, we needed to use an old RS232 cable and a USB converter. Depending on the age of your system, you may need to use an RS232-style connection cord or you may be able to use a USB cable, **11**.

Like most downloads, the software will unpack and install on the PC. Note that JMRI includes several software packages: PanelPro, DecoderPro, and SoundPro. They each serve different parts of the model railroad experience and each is very useful in its category, but for this text we will focus on PanelPro, which is the software intended for defining and operating your layout via a dispatch screen.

Once it is set up and opened for the first time, JMRI will prompt you to connect to the layout. Choose the detection system you are using: this may be the same as your command system (NCE) but may also differ (C/MRI, etc.). Refer to the instruction manual for your system and for JMRI

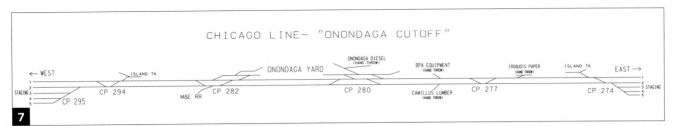

7

A straight-line diagram is critical to signal planning early on.

to get the details correct for your setup. There are also great resources available online for support at JMRI.org or at one of the JMRI usergroups online available through the homepage.

Now that the software is downloaded and set up, you will see several icons as noted previously. We will start with PanelPro. This will be custom for your railroad: you will need one or more hardwired connections from the computer to the railroad depending on your computer, control system, and preferences.

As part of the process through JMRI, you will select the command system you are using and JMRI will automatically name the connection to reflect the manufacturer name.

For the Onondaga Cutoff, I prefer NCE for train control. However, NCE did not have a signal system available in 2013 when signal programming started on the Onondaga Cutoff. Therefore I elected to use Digitrax components to power the signals and switch machines in the interlockings even though I used NCE for block detection.

Setting up a basic Digitrax LocoNet does not require the expense of a new command station. I used the LocoBuffer USB hardware (made by RR-CirKits.com) as the hardware interface between the computer and the Digitrax LocoNet. You need only a Digitrax UP5 and the SE8c signal decoders connected to a parallel command bus to have what is needed to power your interlockings. The translation between NCE and Digitrax is where JMRI comes in.

It may seem counterintuitive that both NCE and Digitrax, with their respective proprietary software and long rivalry, could work together on the same layout. And yet, it is not only possible but smooth. JMRI enables the

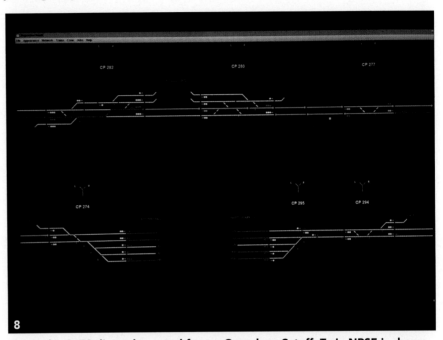

8

This is the CATS dispatcher panel for my Onondaga Cutoff. Train NPSE is shown crossing over from track 2 to track 1 at CP 282 and has a route all the way to CP 274. WAON-10, a local wayfreight, approaches CP 277 on track 2 and will enter Onondaga Yard at CP 280 once NPSE clears.

Onondaga Cutoff to have the reliable train operation, intuitive locomotive consisting, and robust block detection of NCE along with the time-proven Digitrax LocoNet and signaling hardware.

LocoBuffer uses its own software and drivers to talk to the computer, and "translates" between the computer and the command station. The LocoBuffer kit comes with what you need to connect the wiring between the computer and the command system.

If you choose a different setup, such as C/MRI or Layout Command Control (LCC), your interface may be different. Again, each of those systems has extensive manuals and instructions online on the websites or via YouTube. I found working with others who knew more about the system very helpful, and I learned to reach out when I

needed guidance on best practices or needed assistance.

While your hardware and software may differ, the intent is the same—to have the computer talking to the command station before we proceed further. Follow the instructions for your chosen setup to ensure communications are moving between components as needed.

In Chapter 4 we discussed how track occupancy detection is the foundation of a working signal system. It follows that the rest of this chapter is based on robust, reliable detection. The goal of our detection system is to do three things: First; the system must know which detected sections are occupied and which are not. Second, the system must know which detected section on the layout corresponds to the track the system is looking at. Third, and the most critical for us

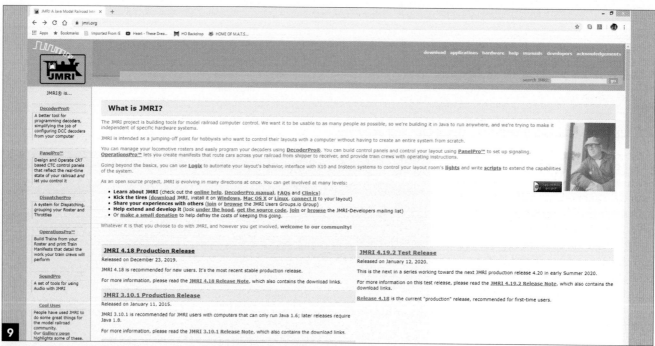

This is the Java Model Railroad Interface (JMRI) home page.

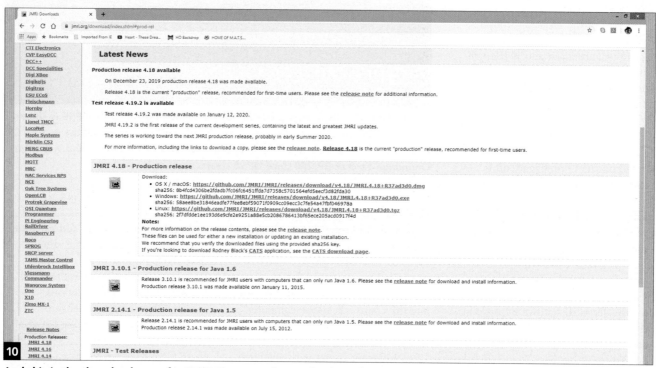

And this is the download page for JMRI. You want the production release to get started.

long term, the system must contain a hard reference that links each unique detected section of track with a unique identifying name or address to physical locations on the layout.

This sounds complicated, but again let's focus on the goal for the system: it needs to know without fail when track is occupied and when it is not, and you need to be able to translate that into specific locations on your railroad.

On the OC, we developed a spreadsheet in Microsoft Excel that allowed us to describe and name each of our 47 blocks so that we had a full list of block names, which in turn allowed us to tell the full signal software which detector refers to which piece of track. The process of naming blocks and assigning sensor numbers will vary depending on the system you have chosen.

In this Excel table, we created a name for the blocks based on their boundary points, which when taken as a pair create a unique name for the block. For example, 280_278_2 (track between CP 280 to intermediate signals at 278, track 2). This is just one way to name blocks. Whichever system you choose, the list becomes your guide. With the list completed, now we need to identify that location for JMRI and keep track of that relationship to simply future maintenance and provide a robust system.

The NCE system by its design determines what the unique identification number will be for each block based on which Automated Input Unit (AIU), and which port, to which it is wired. In NCE only, the identification number is based on the AIU number and pin number. Given those assignments, the system has a preassigned sensor number and that sensor is what is later used to provide input to JMRI for the track occupancy. Refer to the instruction manual for the NCE AIU.

In other words, since each NCE BD20 detector is wired into a certain AIU, and since each AIU has its own cab address (see the AIU instruction manual), each BD20 is uniquely identified by the port through which it is connected to the AIU.

In the Layout Command Control (LCC) and RR-CirKits systems, however, each of these is provided a distinct address from the manufacturer. The user may change it if desired. If so, once you define the user name, it becomes the permanent address of the card. This is a powerful tool that allows lots of flexibility, but for our purposes, while multiple numbers are possible, it is just another way to define what the address should be for each section.

Again, system by system, this process will change—the key is to read directions and pull it together so that certain blocks are named and tied directly to a certain sensor for the software to monitor.

Unique blocks, unique sensor numbers

Next, we need to assign this new hardware address that relates one block to a sensor in JMRI. Sensors are what JMRI uses to follow different parts of the layout and relay the basic "on-off" characteristics of that component to the software that contains the built-in relay logic on which the signal system functions.

If your command station is older, you might need an RS-232 connector like Dave did. The other end has a USB connection to attach it to his computer.

This is where to find the sensors menu.

Each sensor has three sections: the system name (the block detection manufacturer), the hardware address (the unique identifier for that particular section on the layout), and the user name (up to the discretion of the person performing this part of the installation), **12**.

The first step is to open the sensor table in JMRI. Go to the TOOLS menu, choose TABLES, then SENSORS. Press the ADD… button on the bottom of the window. A window opens called the ADD NEW SENSOR window, and you choose the system name (whatever block detection system you are using, defined earlier in the chapter) so as to talk to the address, **13**.

As you can see we have now entered the system name (NCE), the hardware address of 971 (dictated by the AIU port and NCE system in this example, but may be dictated by you the programmer if using LCC or RR-CirKits), and the user name (shown as TEST here, but should be something that associates this with the physical railroad. For the Onondaga Cutoff, as an example, one is named CP280TK2W; this is the block within

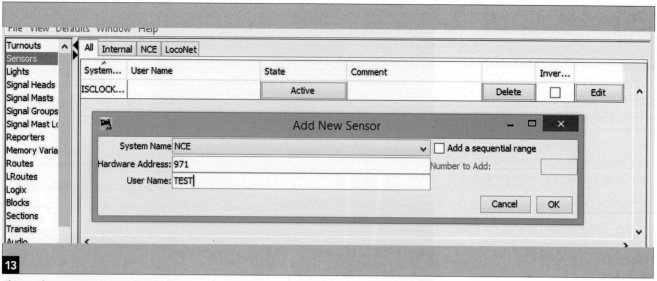

13

This is the ADD NEW SENSOR window.

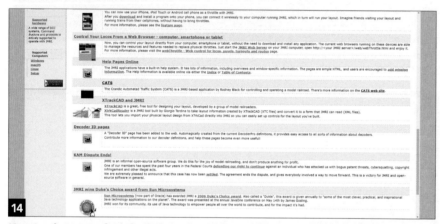

14

Here's where you find the link to the CATS website on the JMRI website.

15

Choose the version of CATS that is compatible with your version of JMRI.

CP 280, on track 2, and is the westernmost of those two blocks.

Now, push OK at the bottom of the window. This will add the new sensor to the table and show the current state of the sensor.

To test this, move a train or car over the newly defined sensor and the applicable section on the layout. You should be able to see the change where the sensor state is shown in the window: ACTIVE versus INACTIVE. If you see UNKNOWN after you have tested, the first step in troubleshooting is to verify again that the detector is working in the field. Make sure it is powered and that the LED on the BD20 will light when the block is occupied by a lit passenger car or locomotive. If the BD20 is working, you likely have a mistake in the process of defining the sensor or in linking it to that particular detector.

Repeat that process as necessary to define each of your block detection sensors.

Installing CATS

Computer Automated Traffic System is the operating library for our working example. It contains much of the programming required to develop operating signals and uses the Windows interface to allow for an ease of building aspects to support your operations. Let's install that next.

From the JMRI home page, scroll down and you will see a link for the CATS home page. This link takes you to the CATS website, **14**.

Once on the CATS page, click on downloads, **15**, and scroll to the bottom. You want to choose the download that is associated with your version of JMRI.

Install CATS per the installation instructions. There are online user support groups with both JMRI and CATS, which enables you as a programmer to communicate directly with experts in each subject as well as in some cases the programmers themselves, an indispensable resource for us as we build the system.

The basic grid square in Designer.

As part of the CATS download, you will also have downloaded the Designer program, which will allow you to program the railroad in JMRI. You can also build the railroad in the computer on JMRI, but that requires starting from scratch and programming the whole thing from the ground up. Computer Automated Traffic System and Designer allows a base set of signal logic and rules to be in place to run the system. The limitation is that CATS offers only the "modern" dispatcher screen.

Building a controlled switch in Designer

Now, it is time to take you through the steps to link these sensors to the physical track on the layout, and our first step there is to build the track diagram in Designer. I will walk you through the process for one powered switch.

This might be the end of a passing siding, the end of a yard installation, or an interlocked junction where one branch joins the main line—but the concept can be expanded to any interlocking. For the purposes of this exercise, we will draw a single switch interlocking similar to fig. **4** on page 91 in Chapter 6 of East Muir on the Montana Rail Link.

As you will recall, this interlocking is the east end of a controlled siding on the former Northern Pacific main line over Bozeman Pass. The siding, to the south, and the main route to the north come back together to run east downhill toward the yard at Livingston, Montana.

Open Designer from the drive on which it was installed, **16**. This provides a format that consists of grid squares. It is formed of rows and columns, so that each grid square

Add rows and columns to build out your track schematic in Designer.

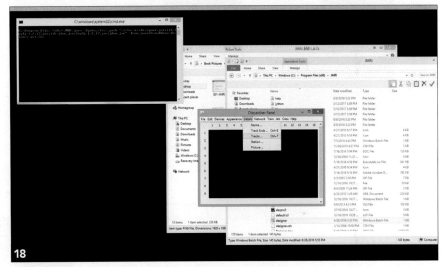

Selecting TRACKS opens a window allowing you to choose track sections.

allows you to build track segments applicable to your track on the layout. It will graphically allow you to add rows and columns so as to allow you to build the track layout at hand, **17**.

Our next step is to draw a track segment. First, we select the DETAILS option from the menu bar in Designer, then TRACKS, **18**.

This opens a SELECT TRACKS window that includes a series of preprogrammed track segments to allow you to create different configurations for your layout, **19**.

All the lines included are either horizontal, vertical, or 45-degree angled slashes to represent switches. Each segment has an adjacent check box; our first move here is to check the horizontal piece, **20**. As you check the segment, the corresponding drop-down

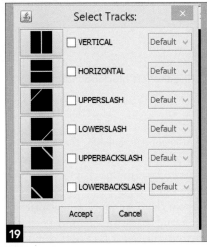

These segments allow you to re-create your track schematic in Designer.

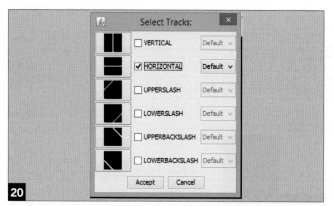

20 The horizontal track segment is checked.

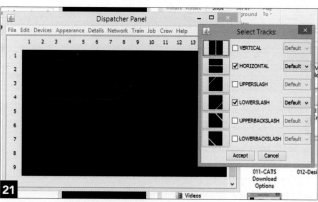

21 Drawing a switch in Designer.

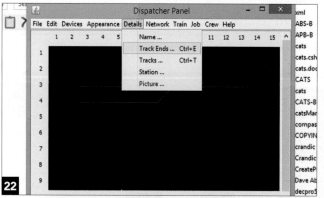

22 TRACK ENDS allows you to define the end of track segments.

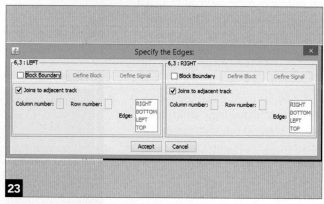

23 The SPECIFY THE EDGES window pops up.

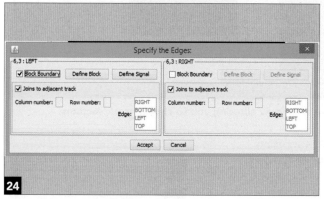

24 Setting the left block boundary.

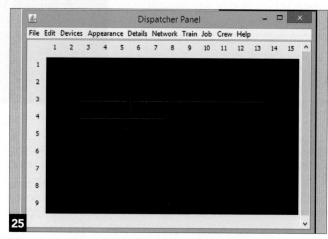

25 The block segment now has a gap showing its end.

menu becomes available. These are the available track speeds and will be discussed later in this chapter when we define signal aspects.

From there, we move to the adjacent square and select the appropriate check box from the SELECT TRACKS menu.

Repeat this process to create the track geometry necessary to define the arrangement of track at this location. In our example of East Muir, that includes horizontals for the main track and the siding. For the switch itself, you will need to select two checkboxes—HORIZONTAL and LOWERSLASH. Note that the "slash" options correspond to the keyboard standard slashes. The only time you need to select more than one checkbox is when you have a switch, diamond, or other intersection, or in certain circumstances of multiple-track main lines, **21**.

Our next step is to link the block detection with the track layout. For our East Muir example, we will first define the location of the insulated joint that defines the interlocking limits at the west end of the interlocking plant. We will start with the main line. The first step is to segment the track layout that we have created in Designer. Highlight the grid square that will be the separation between the track segments. On the menu bar, choose DETAILS, and then TRACK ENDS, **22**.

Now we see the window for defining track ends which Designer calls SPECIFY THE EDGES, **23**.

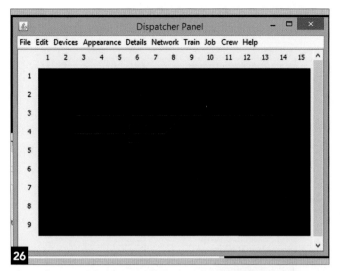

26

The siding now has an insulating gap indicated as well.

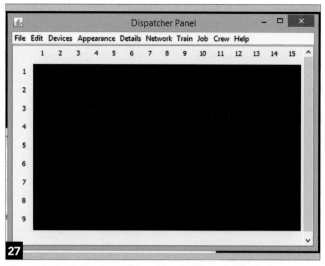

27

The right boundary of the interlocking is defined.

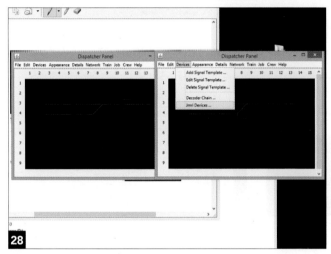

28

Now connect the track section with its corresponding location on the layout.

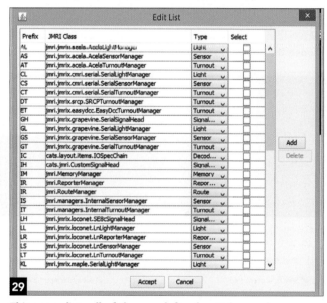

29

This menu lists all of the pre-defined switches and sensors.

Choose on the grid square you selected which end is going to be the division point between the blocks. For horizontals in our example, you can choose the left or right; for verticals Designer allows you to choose top or bottom and for slashes, it is either left or right, and top or bottom to follow the configuration of the slash itself, **24**.

Press ACCEPT to create the block segment, **25**.

For this example, we will use the left boundary of the grid square on the main line to the left of the switch as our insulated joint.

Now we move on to create two more insulated joints. First, create the joint following the steps above for the siding, **26**.

Our final joint is east of the switch at East Muir, and we will define this as a right boundary, **27**.

As you draw the track, be sure to save your work, and then open the file periodically to check how the diagram looks in CATS. There is a bit of trial and error involved in how you build the track diagrams because once the Designer file translates to CATS, the diagram is a bit smaller. Some experimentation may be needed as you get used to the system, especially when replicating more complicated interlockings to scale them to the screen.

Now we have our interlocking isolated from the surrounding track in Designer, which represents the

insulated joints on the prototype and on the layout. Now that the interlocking is delineated with defined limits, we can associate each track section in Designer with the actual track section on the layout.

The first step is to tell Designer what block detection system we are using. From the menu bar, choose the DEVICES menu, and select JMRI DEVICES, **28**.

The menu will open, with all the available JMRI classes of pre-defined sensors, switches, etc that are available in the program, **29**.

From this list, you will select which block detection system you are using. For example, for NCE BD20s, you choose NS from the far left column,

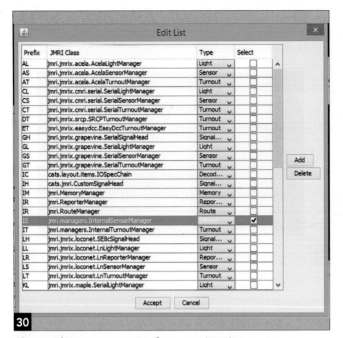

30

Choose the correct sensor for your situation.

31

And choose the correct turnout control.

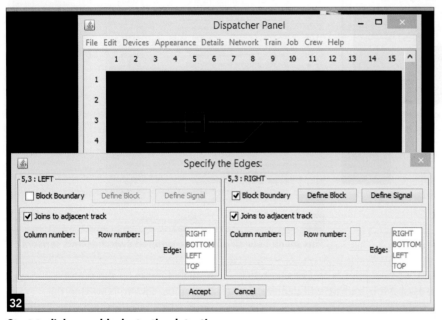

32

Start to link your blocks to the detection sensor.

33

This menu allows for naming the blocks on the schematic.

defined in the adjacent column. For C/MRI, you would choose CS; for Digitrax you should choose LS (LocoNet Sensor), and so on, **30**.

For this exercise we will choose IS which stands for INTERNAL SENSOR in JMRI, since we are not tied to an actual layout. If you are actually building this interlocking on a layout, choose your block-detection manufacturer.

Note that this JMRI DEVICES table is also used to define turnout control. While this box is open, let's also tell Designer what your turnout control

will be. The same procedure follows for turnout control as for block control. Simply check the box next to your turnout control system. If Digitrax, select LT (LocoNet Turnout). NT would be NCE turnout control. Press ACCEPT, **31**.

It is normal for more than one box to be checked and that check boxes for different systems make no difference to JMRI. With the track all set via the PanelPro and Designer applications, we get to see the remarkable versatility of the JMRI platform.

After all this is defined, it is time to link your block detection to the track segment. (We will link the turnout later.) In our example, we have four blocks. Whichever block section you choose first, highlight one edge of that section in the grid. Go back to DETAILS and select TRACK ENDS. The block boundary should already be checked, based on what we selected earlier, **32**.

Since we are on the right in this example, we should note that the right side of the insulated joint in one grid square is the same edge as the left side of the insulated joint in the adjacent grid square to the right. Either can be used for this definition. Click on the DEFINE BLOCK button. This opens a DESCRIBE DETECTION BLOCK window, where we can input information, 33.

We see here the block name and station. Refer to the current CATS manual for how these are defined and for suggestions on what to input. For this example, we will name our four blocks. The names for your layout should be what you named the blocks in Chapter 4. For this example, we will use B1, B2, B3, and B4; with B1 as the main line west of the plant, B2 as the siding west of the plant, B3 as the plant itself, and B4 as the main east of the plant. The station name is not necessary but is helpful. Again, the CATS manual will provide guidance on how to proceed.

Continuing in the DESCRIBE DETECTION BLOCK window, we will now move to include signal design. This is where we define whether our control is CTC, or ABS; or going further APB, etc. Again, the CATS manual will be critical to define how the signal system works in the software. For our example we will select CTC.

We now need to tie the block detection address to the track layout in Designer. There are two parts of the bottom part of the window: OCCUPIED REPORT and UNOCCUPIED REPORT. What address and status will each use to report occupied or unoccupied?

For each slot, select the drop down, and choose the appropriate system. For our example, this will be IS for internal sensor; for your layout that may be different as discussed previously.

Here, we input the hardware address. For most systems the occupied and unoccupied address will be the same. However, some systems may exist where you have different statuses. For both NCE and Digitrax, OCCUPIED is defined as CLOSE, and UNOCCUPIED is defined as THROW. In our East Muir example, we are using IS for internal sensor, with OCCUPIED defined as CLOSE for B1, and with UNOCCUPIED defined as THROW for B1. Press ACCEPT in the DESCRIBE DETECTION BLOCK window, and press ACCEPT again in the SPECIFY THE EDGES window, 34.

The block you have been working on will change color in Designer to white. This shows that in our defined CTC rules, this track is ready for testing, 35.

Now, follow the above for the other three blocks. As you complete each

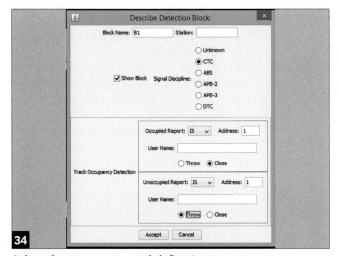

34 Select the sensor type and define its states.

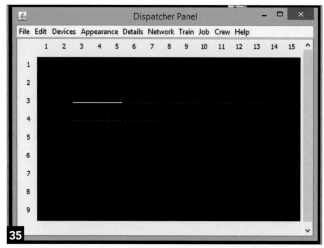

35 With the information saved, the segment turns white.

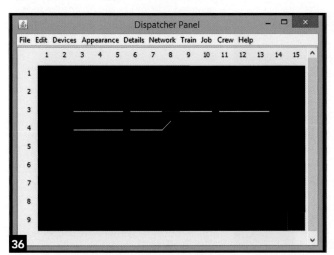

36 All blocks are defined, except the switch.

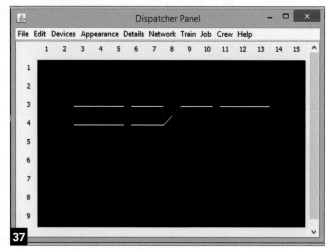

37 The switch needs a little more attention.

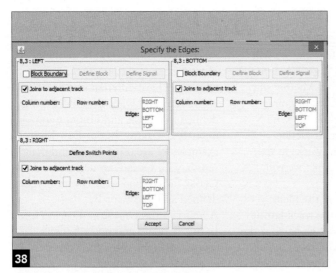

38

This time, choose DEFINE SWITCH POINTS.

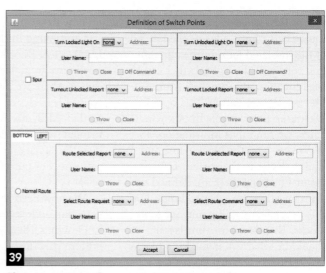

39

The orientation of our switch is bottom left.

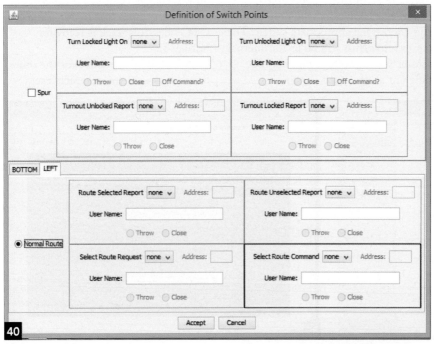

40

The left route is defined as "normal," the straight route through the turnout.

41

Choose the switch type, then assign its address.

block each should turn white. Once all are defined we see all the blocks in our example showing as white lines, **36**.

Why is the switch showing red? Because that requires another definition. Let's do that now.

Defining the switch—normal or reverse

Normal and reverse are terms we commonly hear on the railroad in the Communications & Signals department. For us in JMRI, those terms equate to close and throw. Computer Automated Traffic System uses both—you're defining the normal route in order to start this process. On the prototype, normal usually means straight, but that is not guaranteed: for our sample, we will use the standard definition and nomenclature—normal (close) is the straight route, and reversed (throw) is the diverging route.

Continuing in Designer, highlight the cell that contains the switch itself, **37**.

Click on the Menu bar, then DEFINE TRACK ENDS, **38**.

This brings up the SPECIFY THE EDGES window. We have seen this before for block boundaries, but now you will use a different button—the DEFINE SWITCH POINTS button. Click on that. Now we see the DEFINITION OF SWITCH POINTS window, **39**.

There are a top and bottom half to this window as shown. We are working with the bottom half here. Check your Designer manual. In short, the two legs of the turnout each correlate to a side of the grid square that contains the switch points on your screen. In our example, that is the bottom, and the left side.

In every example, one of these needs to be defined as the normal route for the turnout. In our case, the left side is normal, as it is the straight and the dominant route. This definition is up to you, and can be defined for your situation.

For our example, click on the bottom half of the window and choose the LEFT tab. Select that as the Normal route, **40**.

This data is input the same way we assigned a sensor to a block—we will assign a turnout in JMRI to the switch points in Designer. We now populate the ROUTE SELECTED REPORT and the SELECT ROUTE COMMAND fields, **41**.

As seen at left, from the drop-down menu you choose the hardware IT (for "internal turnout," you may select otherwise for your example—if using a Digitrax SE8c and turnout as installed in the previous chapter, define accordingly), then you input the turnout address (again, specific to your layout). Now we input the user name (optional) and then select CLOSE—in Designer, CLOSE relates to the normal route, **42**.

Above right we see the completed ROUTE SELECTION REPORT. Replicate this same process for the SELECT ROUTE COMMAND in the DEFINITION OF SWITCH POINTS window as seen at right, **43**.

Now we have completed the normal side of the turnout, and the window appears as in **44**:

For the Reverse side of the switch, we go to the BOTTOM tab on the bottom half of the DEFINITION OF SWITCH POINTS window. The bottom tab is used as the route passes through the bottom of the cell on the screen as seen. The procedure is the same for the normal route, but instead of choosing CLOSE you will choose THROW. The screen below shows the reverse side completed, **45**.

In the DEFINITION OF SWITCH POINTS window press ACCEPT. After that, in the SPECIFY THE EDGES

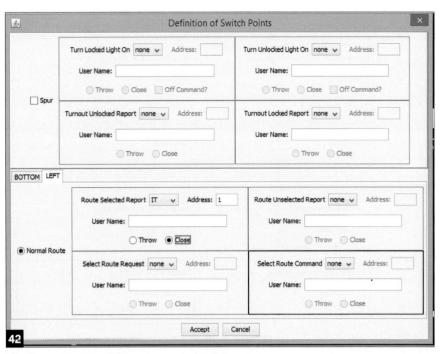

The ROUTE SELECTED REPORT is now complete.

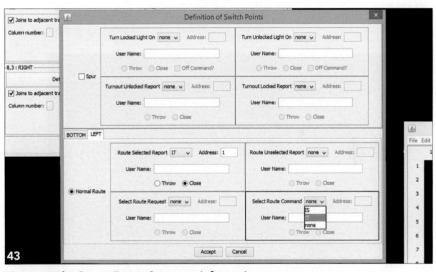

Next, set the SELECT ROUTE COMMAND information.

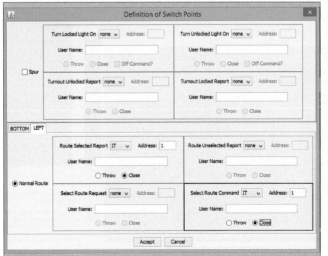

44

The normal route through the turnout is defined.

117

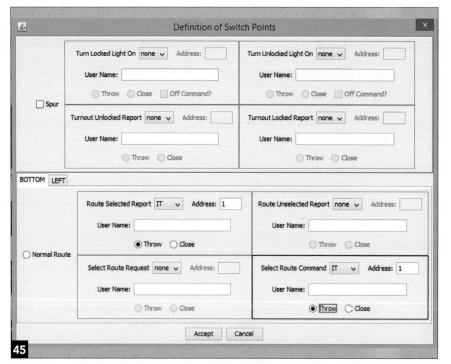

45

The reverse route through the turnout is now defined.

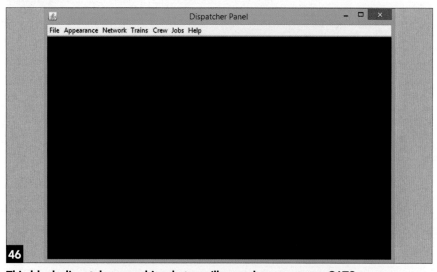

46

This blank dispatcher panel is what you'll see when you open CATS.

47

Use FILE/OPEN to get to the schematic you drew.

window, also press ACCEPT.

At this point, save the file—and as with all digital processes, make it a habit to save on a regular basis.

OK, take a deep breath—you've reached a point where we can open this file in CATS and JMRI and test the whole shebang: actual block detection and the turnout control. Signals will come next.

Testing the controlled switch

Open CATS, which in turn will also open JMRI. Your layout should also be turned on at this time. When you open CATS, you will see a blank dispatcher panel window, **46**.

Go to FILE and OPEN and navigate to your designer file that you recently saved, **47**.

Open the file. It will load and you should see the turnout with associated blocks. If this file does not load or CATS doesn't open properly, consult the CATS manual, and review the previous procedures, **48**.

You should see the panel above. If you do, congratulations! At this point, you should be able to throw the turnout on the layout from the panel by clicking on the points. Further, if you occupy your block with a lit passenger car, locomotive, or resistive-wheelset car, it should trigger the track occupancy light on the screen.

The final step in creating the track template is to define track speeds. In CATS, the signal aspects are dependent on the speed of the track as assigned in Designer. While these are listed as SPEEDS this does not limit your approach of either "speed" or "route" signaling: this is simply the method CATS uses for you to define your signals in the software. Therefore each track segment must have an assigned speed of one of the following: NORMAL, LIMITED, MEDIUM, or SLOW. DEFAULT is also available but is not a definition once we move to defining aspects in the next section.

Each piece of the route in Designer should have a speed assigned to it. I will show you the turnout, and the same methodology works for each block you create in Designer.

First, highlight the switch points.

When that cell is selected, go to DETAILS and then TRACKS. This will open the SELECT TRACKS window, which we have seen before, **49**.

From here you can assign a speed to the normal and reverse legs of the turnout. In the SELECT TRACKS window, look to the right, you can see where you can input the speed from the drop down menu, **50**.

We will assign the horizontal line NORMAL, which is the normal route for the turnout. Now assign the lowerslash as shown as MEDIUM. You could do LIMITED, or SLOW; this is entirely up to you based on your layout geometry and how you want this to be defined according to the prototype. Your railroad's rulebook will include appropriate speeds for diverging moves, defining each as normal, limited, medium, or slow speeds. The rulebook is a handy reference when defining speeds here, **51**.

Now hit ACCEPT. Save the file.

Any non-diverging sections should be listed as NORMAL for our purposes. Now, go through all the remaining cells and define all the sections as described above.

Defining signals

We have finally come to it—defining signals for your interlocking. Signals come in many shapes and sizes. They look considerably different. Some have one light; some have many. Some are even a semaphore blade.

For different units, you the modeler are living in a golden age: most of what you need to model these different systems is available commercially from several manufacturers. Further, like the prototype, different manufacturers specialize in different systems. For modelers looking to install color light signals, you can use most any manufacturer's system. For modelers looking to replicate PRR Position Lights, N&W Position Lights, or B&O Color Position Lights, for example, the system made by RR-CirKits offers specific directions on how to program these aspects using their hardware.

Specifically, the Signalman product produced by RR-CirKits offers specific wiring and programming examples

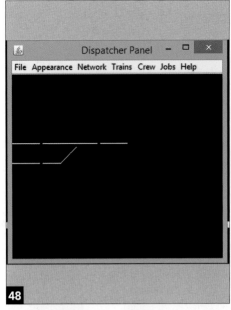

48

The open schematic appears!

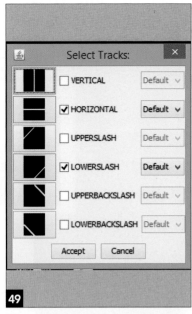

49

Next, define speeds in each block.

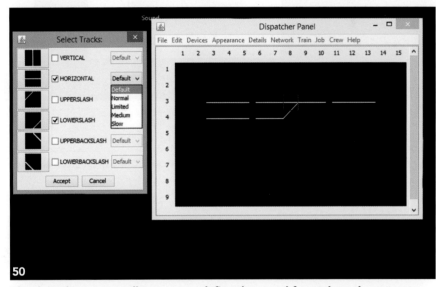

50

The drop-down menu allows you to define the speed for each track segment.

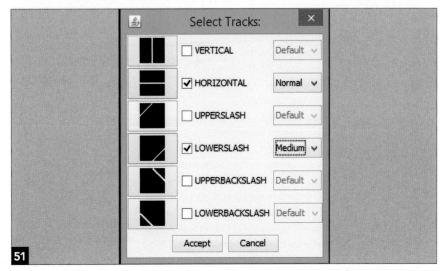

51

Railroad rule books offer information on allowable speeds through turnout routes.

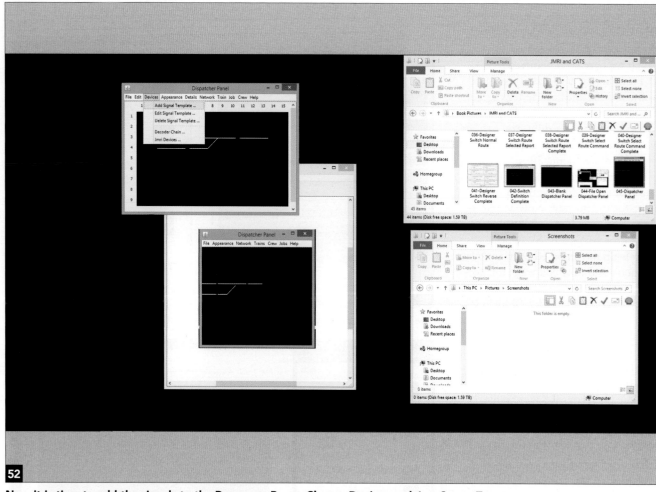

52

Now it is time to add the signals to the Dispatcher Panel. Choose Devices and Add Signal Template.

Naming signals

Railroads have a strong tendency to name each and every track, switch, and building. This also includes signals, which are named according to a standard procedure on each prototype railroad. While each railroad has its own particularities, each is consistent across signals so as to maintain their own standard that is acceptable to the Federal Railway Administration (FRA), which has codes and authoritative regulations to ensure safety. On most railroads, signal names include the location and a track designation. Signals are named with even numbers and the direction they govern, to differentiate them from switches which in turn are named with odd numbers. So for example, a simple interlocking will include names like 2E, 2W, and 4E as noted in the diagram. These should be included in your CATS programming for reference by users and during maintenance.

Further, automatic signals carry a number plate, which is considered part of the signal aspect for crews and also

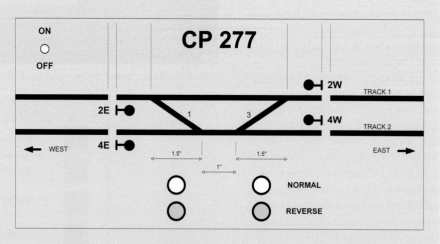

are generally labeled with location info. For example, the numberplate may read 2981W. On Conrail, and predecessors NYC and PRR, this would signify an automatic signal within mile 298, on track 1, governing the westward movement.

for position lights in their manual (rr-cirkits.com/manuals/SignalMan-manual-c.pdf) The logic can be delivered by what we have learned in this chapter already, but the aspects are determined by the signal decoders themselves.

Likewise, semaphore signals use the same logic, but instead of just wiring lights we also need to wire a slow-motion machine such as a Tortoise-brand switch machine to drive the blade position. The Digitrax SE8c and the RR-CirKits Switchman both have specific instructions on the procedures for installing working semaphore signals.

Other examples exist and the message to you is this: use the resources described in this text as a framework to guide research on the internet to determine which manufacturer is a good choice for your chosen path. Some modelers like wiring, and would rather wire than program. Some favor programming over wiring. With different products available there is no one-size-fits-all approach: your desired system will likely benefit from some homework on the available products that most benefit your vision.

For the purposes of this example, we will proceed with instructions to wire 3-color LED searchlights (or three-light signals with three separate LEDs). Note that bi-color LEDs that

can be used to approximate the look of 3-color units will have slightly different wiring.

Let's dig in to the 3-color LED example. Go to DEVICES and ADD SIGNAL template, **52**.

This will open the EDIT SIGNAL template as seen below, **53**.

Here we will define the signal name (1W, which stands for "one west") and we will define two heads. Here you can choose LAMP or SEMAPHORE. (For the differences, check the CATS manual.)

We are using lamps, **54**.

Click the CREATE ASPECTS button to open the SIGNAL ASPECTS TEMPLATE.

From the start, you can see this table is populated. It grays out speeds you haven't defined, and shows colors for your signal heads depending on route and occupancy. In each of the table's cells you can see two colors; this equates to your top and bottom signal heads. This allows the signal to be lit once we wire it in the next section. The

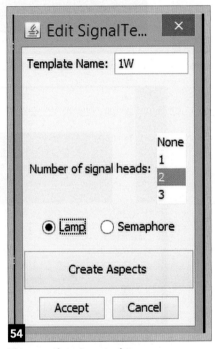

This is the EDIT SIGNAL TEMPLATE.

The template is complete.

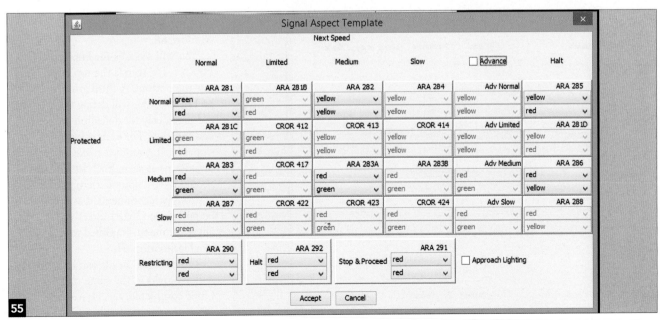

The SIGNAL ASPECT TEMPLATE will be populated based on the decisions you made earlier. Choose ACCEPT.

		Normal	Limited	Medium	Slow	Advance	Halt
Protected	Normal	ARA 281: green / red	ARA 281B: green / red	ARA 282: yellow / yellow	ARA 284: yellow / yellow	Adv Normal: yellow / yellow	ARA 285: yellow / red
	Limited	ARA 281C: green / red	CROR 412: green / red	CROR 413: yellow / yellow	CROR 414: yellow / yellow	Adv Limited: yellow / yellow	ARA 281D: yellow / red
	Medium	ARA 283: red / green	CROR 417: red / green	ARA 283A: red / green	ARA 283B: red / green	Adv Medium: red / green	ARA 286: red / yellow
	Slow	ARA 287: red / green	CROR 422: red / green	CROR 423: red / green	CROR 424: red / green	Adv Slow: red / green	ARA 288: red / yellow

Restricting — ARA 290: red / red   Halt — ARA 292: red / red   Stop & Proceed — ARA 291: red / red   ☐ Approach Lighting

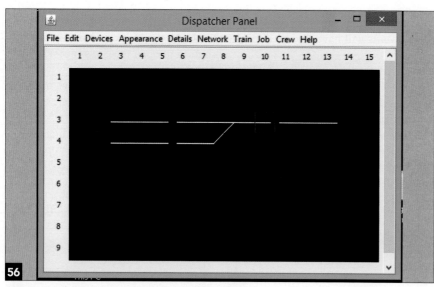

Select a signal location on the Dispatcher Panel.

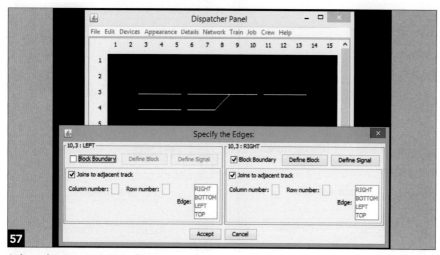

Select the DEFINE SIGNAL button.

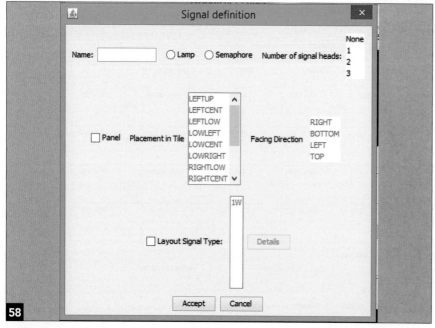

In the SIGNAL DEFINITION window, we'll choose LAMP and 2 for signal heads.

CATS manual will cover the details of this table, **55**.

Press ACCEPT in each of the windows, and your template is created.

Now, we are going to place a signal on the dispatcher screen to relate to the signal on the layout. Select the cell where you want the signal placed, **56**.

Choose the DETAILS menu and TRACK ENDS. This will again bring up the SPECIFY THE EDGES window. Select the DEFINE SIGNAL button, **57**.

This will bring up the SIGNAL DEFINITION window, **58**.

Choose LAMP and the number of signal heads (two for our example). If you want the signal visible on your panel (for all controlled signals), you will choose the panel button. You can place the signal on the tile where you please. This is generally to the right of the train in the direction the signal faces. So, I used UPLEFT which puts the signal above the track. Since the signal governs movements to the left (west for our example), select the FACING DIRECTION menu and choose LEFT. Where the signal is drawn does not need to correlate to the location on the layout, however, closer is better for operational purposes.

On the bottom of this window, check the layout signal type box, and select the template you wish to use. In our case there is only one at this point, **59**.

Click DETAILS. This brings up the SIGNAL HEAD DEFINITIONS window, **60**.

You will see tabs for HEAD 0 and HEAD 1. HEAD 0 is the top head, HEAD 1 is the bottom. A third lower would be HEAD 2. We will define these as we did previously for detection sections and turnouts. For each color on each signal head, you must make separate definitions as seen. Each signal head should have a unique username. This is strongly recommended as it will be pulled into JMRI directly and allow for much simplified testing and troubleshooting, **61**.

Other signal heads can be created and assigned in the same manner. Once completed, the HEAD 1 definition looks like this, **62**:

And now our designer panel

appears as follows, **63**:

It is recommended to do one signal at a time. Test it and get it working, and move on—it is easier to troubleshoot one at a time. You can open each and load to test through CATS. The best way to test is to test each of the signal lamp colors separately before you test the whole aspect using multiple heads.

Use the SIGNAL HEADS table in JMRI. You should see each of your signals in the table with the username that you input. Cycle through the colors and test each to ensure the wiring is correct and the programming works.

As you can see, the unique naming of signal heads and turnouts in the field is central to the operation of the system. Good record keeping will help ensure minimal confusion as you move forward. Repeat as necessary for each and every head on your layout.

And, as you go through the process, you will be able to "cut in" interlockings one by one by working on heads one interlocking at a time.

Conclusions

As of this writing in the spring of 2020, we are seeing new opportunities for prototype signaling. The National Model Railroad Association standards for Layout Command Control (LCC) are gaining traction with all the benefits of modern programming and more flexible hardware.

Java Model Railroad Interface itself continues to develop, including LCC and interfaces with other manufacturer's hardware. Digital Command Control is at this time solidly accepted in train control, but the horizon is bright with battery power for trains as well as different control interfaces such as WiThrottle and other mobile-device-based options.

Railroading, like model railroading, is changing. But, like our prototype, the hobby still at its core is about making something work and pulling the people and resources together that we need to make that happen, **64**. There is a lot of good railroading left, and more good modeling every day. By coming together in that light you have

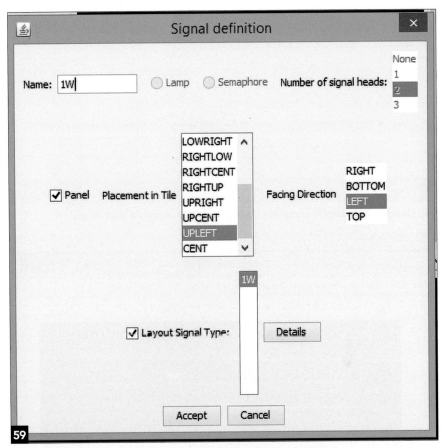

59

Check the LAYOUT SIGNAL TYPE box and choose the signal type.

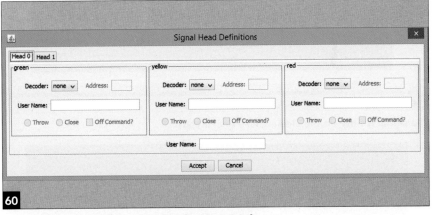

60

Define the top signal head under the HEAD 0 tab.

61

The definition for signal head 0 is complete.

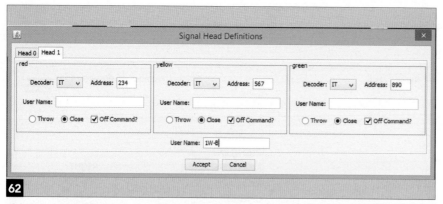

62

The Head 1 definition is complete. Don't forget to assign a user name.

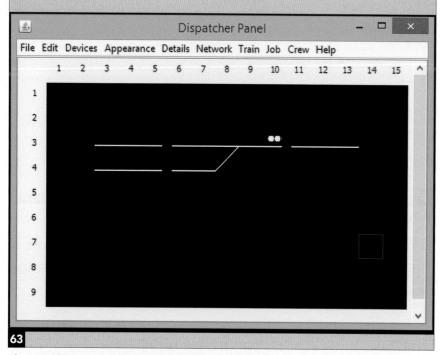

63

The signal is now on the Dispatcher Panel layout.

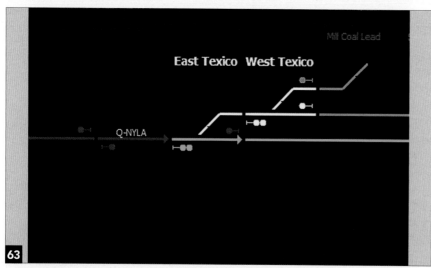

63

The Q-LANY, a hot eastbound UPS piggyback train, is lined straight through West Texico interlocking on Sammy Carlisle's ATSF Hereford Sub. This view is using the CATS software. *Sammy Carlile*

a chance to make something that will help make memories for a lifetime.

The grand thing about our hobby as it grows and changes is that there are always more options on how to better accomplish signaling. But the basics remain: robust detection, operations planning for prototypical interlocking design, and good construction techniques will continue to be the foundation upon which any effective system is built.

Modeling railroading is an active endeavor, and it explores so much of the human experience in our minds, and in the minds of others. Signaling helps bring a layout to life, lending motion, action and authenticity to your modeled reality. You have an opportunity to create something remarkable that can bring people together: in effect, joining in the energy of what the prototype railroads were created to do. Building something with that capacity helps to bridge differences and can be a foundation for community going forward.

We've learned a lot in this book: the origin of signaling, different systems and why they came to be, basics of design and construction, and finally installation and programming a working signal system. This work, however, is not exhaustive nor exclusive: there are many ways to get to the goal. This one, however, was designed and engineered by professionals and has worked for me. Without a doubt, the foundation is solid, and the system in total has proven robust for nearly a decade. Now you, too, can look back at your progress with some new understanding of a prototype system we have distilled down to work for your layout. Your fun is just beginning!

64
Santa Fe 502 west rolls under the cantilever signal bridge in Hereford at dusk
with a hotshot train. The signal bridge is an N.J. International kit and the signal
heads are by BLMA. There are 12 wires that run down the center mast of the
signal bridge. Sammy Carlisle's Hereford Sub is a snapshot of the Atchison,
Topeka & Santa Fe in the golden days of its independence in the early 1990s.
There is a lot of great railroading still out there. *Sammy Carlile*

Appendix:
Scratchbuilding mechanical interlocking and signal controls

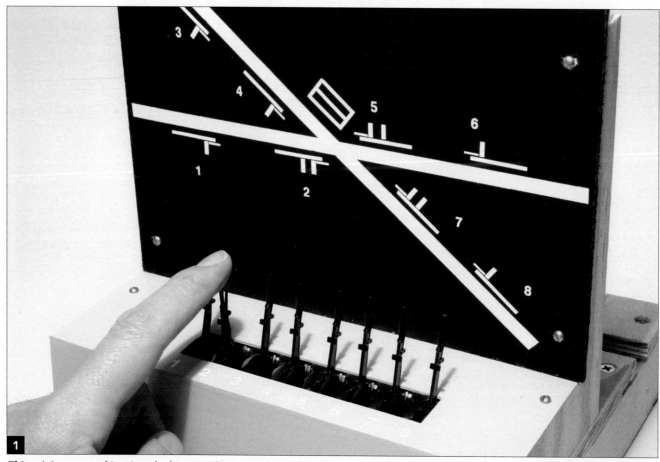

This miniature working interlocking machine uses Hump Yard Purveyance levers and a styrene strip locking bed to control signals at a crossing.

These techniques, from Jeff Wilson's *The Model Railroader's Guide to Junctions*, provide a couple of alternate methods of controlling signals and switch machines. Especially for transition-era modelers, this appendix may hold the keys for interlockings on your layout.

Wherever real railroads cross or multiple routes meet at junctions, some type of control is needed to keep two trains from trying to occupy the same part of the track. The control system for a junction or crossing is called an interlocking, and consists of all of the signals and turnout controls for that area—all of which are tied together, or interlocked, to prevent conflicting routes from being selected.

Interlockings are fascinating places to model.

One option is computerized control. However, it's possible—and easier than you might think—to model a fully functional mechanical interlocking, **1**, where several control levers are physically interlocked with each other to control working signals and switch machines. We'll take you through the steps of doing just that.

If you don't want the complexity of a working interlocking, you still can control signals and switches in a realistic manner using

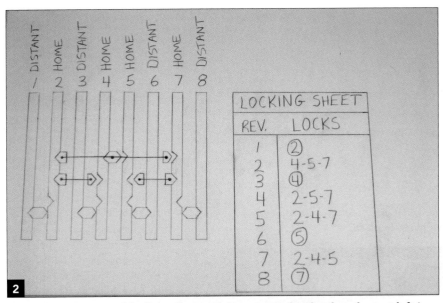

2 The locking sheet at right lists what each lever must do; the dog chart at left is a pattern for the tappets (vertical bars) and locking bars and dogs (horizontal bars).

3 The Hump Yard lever kits are molded in engineering plastic, with several types of mounting bases and optional parts included.

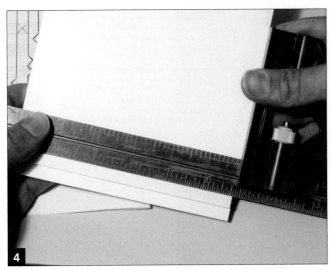

4 Glue the bottom locking bar guide strip in place, making sure it is square to the base.

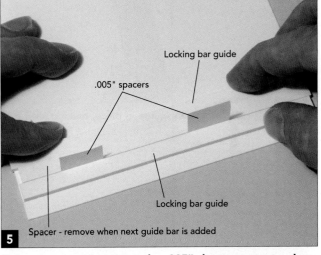

5 Use a styrene strip spacer plus .005" sheet spacers to place the next locking bar guide strip.

Centralized Traffic Control (CTC) style control levers, or you can simply use toggle, slide, or rotary switches. We'll take a look at several available options.

Dog charts

The key to building a working mechanical interlocking is an accurate locking sheet and dog chart. The locking sheet is a logic list of what each control lever must do. The dog chart shows how the tappets (the numbered bars connected to the control levers) and locking bars with dogs (the bars perpendicular to the tappets) must be arranged to follow the locking sheet.

The locking sheet and dog chart for the simple crossing in **1** are shown in **2**. Each signal, switch, derail, and lock in an interlocking is numbered (although there are only signals in this example). The possible signals are limited, as there's only a crossing and no alternate routes, making this interlocking easy to build. Signals are normally at stop: red for distant signals, and red-over-red (with a permanent lower red) for home signals. Clearing a route will give a green distant signal and green-over-red home signal.

On the locking sheet, the numbers down the left column match these numbered components and corresponding levers. The second column shows the levers that must be locked when the lever in the first column is reversed (a circle around a number means that it must be locked in reverse).

The chart is a series of logic (if x, then y) statements. The control levers at an interlocking must be thrown in a specific order: First is turnouts, then switch locks, home signal,

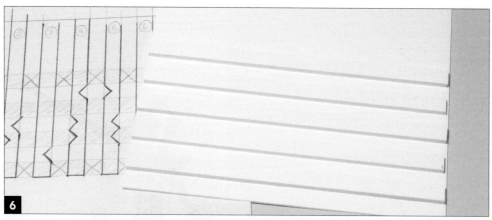

6

All of the locking bar guide strips are shown glued in place.

7

Glue the left-side tappet-bar guide in place, making sure it is perpendicular to the locking-bar guide strips.

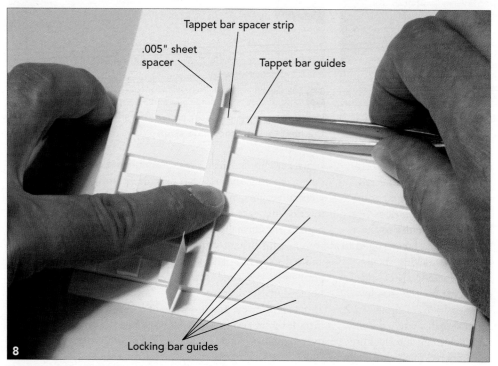

.005" sheet spacer

Tappet bar spacer strip

Tappet bar guides

Locking bar guides

8

Short lengths of .125" x .312" strips serve as tappet bar guides. Make sure they don't hang over the slots between the locking bar guides.

and distant signal. Since there are no turnouts in this plan, the order is simply home signal, then distant signal.

For example, for this crossing, clearing (reversing) any of the home signals should lock out all of the other home signals. Thus, on the locking sheet, reversing lever 2 (which sets that home signal to clear) locks levers 4, 5, and 7 (the other three home signals). Reversing lever 1 (which sets that route's corresponding distant signal to clear) then locks lever 2 in position—no other moves are possible unless levers 1 and 2 are moved back to their normal positions.

Applying this to the dog chart, you can see that reversing lever/tappet 2 (pushing it down one bar width) will push the top locking bar out of its notch in lever 2 and into notches in tappets 5 and 7, locking them, and will push the lower locking bar into the notch on tappet 4, locking it.

Let's walk through building an interlocking frame step-by-step, based on the above junction. Doing so will demonstrate how the logic of the locking sheet and dog chart works, and will help you in planning other interlockings.

Building the frame

Once you have established the dog chart, you can begin building the frame. I suggest drawing the pattern for the tappets and locking bars full size. I built my model in similar fashion as Gordy Odegard did in building a working interlocking, which he described in the January through March 1961 issues of *Model Railroader*. (Don

Ball built a similar machine, described in the January and February 2015 issues.)

In his original model, Gordy used heavy strip brass for the frame, tappets, and locking bars. This made the model extremely rugged, but also quite challenging and time-consuming to build. I used strip styrene to build my locking bed, and although styrene isn't as strong as brass, it has proven to work quite well. A stronger alternative is ABS plastic from Plastruct.

The other key components are the miniature armstrong levers made by Hump Yard Purveyance, **3**. The Hump Yard products are beautiful, large-scale models that resemble prototype levers. The kits also include actuating wire and mounting hardware. Hump Yard is out of business, but you might find the levers at train shows or online secondhand.

The levers can be mounted in several configurations. I used a flat locking bed and mounted the levers flat in front of the bed, but you can alter this to fit your available space. You can

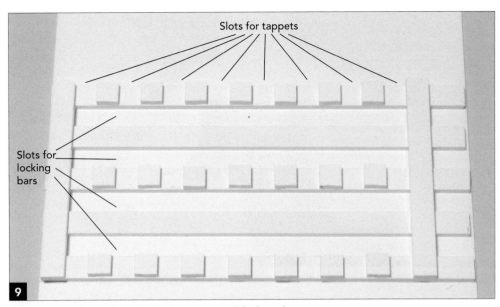

9 The finished frame is ready for tappets and locking bars.

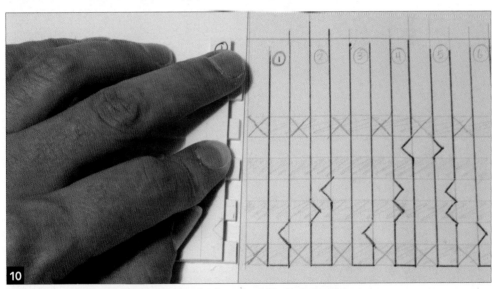

10 Mark the notches on each tappet following the full-sized template.

11 A hobby knife works to cut the notches, but it's difficult to keep the angle of the notch square and the edges of the cut vertical.

12 Micro-Mark's Corner Punch (no. 81652) works well for cutting notches. The inner point of the notch should be at the halfway point of the strip width.

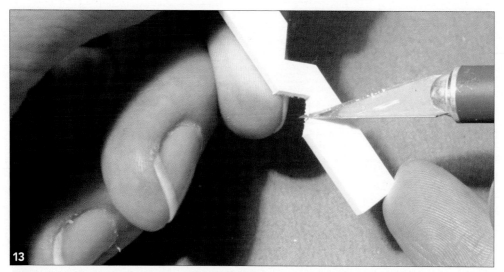

13

Remove any flash or stray material from the edges of each notch.

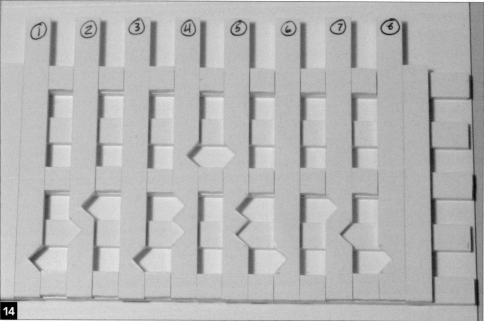

14

The completed tappets are in place in their slots in the frame.

15

Dogs are made by gluing wedge-shaped pieces of styrene on top of the .125" x .312" locking bars. Label each locking bar so you know where it goes in the frame.

16

Cut a pointed end on a styrene strip with a hobby knife or NorthWest Short Line Chopper.

make the panel free-standing, 1, build it into your layout's fascia, or come up with another mounting scheme.

The levers and locking frame enable you to control signals and turnouts either directly by use of actuating wire connected to the tappets, or with electrical slide switches connected to the tappets. More on that later.

Start with a sheet of .040" or heavier styrene for the base. The dimensions should be larger than those of the frame components (I goofed and made mine a bit too short—remember it's easy to trim it later if it's too big). Make sure all edges of the base are cut at 90-degree angles. Use liquid plastic cement to glue the first horizontal locking bar guide piece in place, 4. These pieces, the locking bars, and the tappets are all .125" x .312" styrene strips (Evergreen no. 390). I found this size to be sturdy enough for the job but still thin enough to cut and work with easily.

The frame must be square to work properly, so check each piece with a square as they're glued in place, 4. Use a .125" x .312" styrene strip as a spacer in positioning each succeeding guide piece, but with an additional .005" styrene spacer to make sure the locking bar will be able to slide freely in the slot, **5**. As each new guide piece is added, place a styrene strip in the resulting slot and check that it can move freely. Repeat until all of the crosspieces are in place, **6**.

Glue the left-side tappet-bar guide piece (also .125" x .312") into place, **7**, once again making sure that it is square to the horizontal guide pieces. The pieces that guide the intermediate tappet bars are short lengths of .125" x .312" styrene placed on the top, middle, and bottom horizontal guides. Glue these in place, **8**, using another .125" x .312" strip plus a .005" spacer to align them. Use the square to ensure they are perpendicular to the horizontal pieces, **9**.

Tappets and locking bars

Cut eight tappets from .125" x .312" strip to the same length. I cut mine so that in the normal position they're even with the bottom of the lower horizontal guide and ¾" above the top guide (where they will meet the levers). Set them in place and make sure they move freely in their slots. Use a permanent marker to label them with their numbers.

Starting with tappet no. 1, follow the full-size template and dog chart and mark the lever where it is to be cut by setting it in place atop the frame. Make sure its bottom is even with the edge of the bottom locking bar guide strip, **10**. Use a pencil to mark the tappet. The top and

The completed dog or dogs should have a minimal amount of play. Test each as they're built.

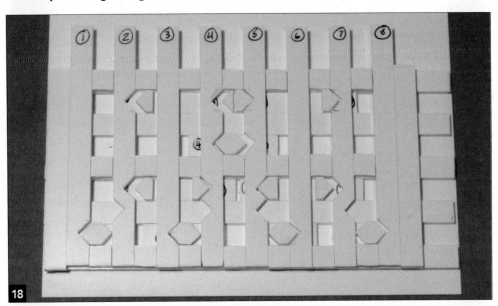

All locking bars are in place and tappets are in their normal positions, ready for testing.

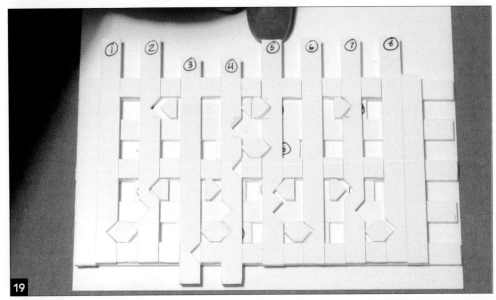

With tappets 3 and 4 reversed, tappet 5 can't move—the dogs are properly locking out all other tappets.

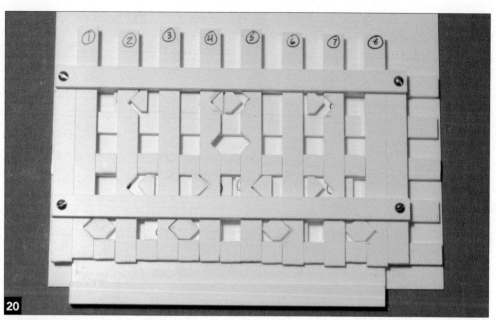

20

Use screws to secure a pair of strips across the tappets to hold them in place. Glue a strip across the bottom to act as a stop for the tappets in the reversed position.

bottom of each notch should align with its corresponding horizontal locking bar slot.

You can use a chisel-tip hobby knife to cut the notches, **11**, but a Micro-Mark corner cutter (item no. 81652) will be much faster, **12**. The corner cutter can be mounted in a drill press (not turning). Pulling down on the press handle cuts the notch. The result is a perfect 90-degree cut every time.

Use a hobby knife to clean any flash or jagged edges from the notch, **13**, then place the tappet back in the frame to make sure it moves freely in its slot. The

completed tappets in place in the frame are shown in **14**.

Let's move to the dogs. You can see a few completed dogs in **15**. Cut a 90-degree pointed end on a .125" x .312" strip, **16**, trim the end from the strip, and glue it on top of a .125" x .312" styrene strip locking bar.

The dimensions of the dogs are critical to the function of the locking bed. Use the tappets as your measuring guide, and test each dog and locking bar as they're completed to make sure they fit properly. They shouldn't fit snugly—leave just a bit of play, but not

much more than 1⁄32" or the lever will be able to move too much. You can see the proper fit of the small dog between tappets 1 and 2 in **17**.

Photo **18** shows all of the tappets and locking bars in place, with the tappets in their normal positions. Now's the time to play with the locking bed, both to get a feel for how the system works and to make sure the levers lock each other out as they should.

Test all possible lever combinations. In **19** you can see that tappets 3 and 4 are reversed, and it shows that tappet no. 5 (and all other

tappets) can't be moved. All of the dogs are doing their jobs, locking into their respective notches. Make sure that all of the tappets and locking bars operate smoothly before moving to the next steps.

During testing, I discovered that the second locking bar from the top was unnecessary (which is reflected in the dog chart in **2**. Note that later photos have this locking bar removed.

Once the parts are working properly, add two styrene strips across the tappets to hold them in position, **20**. Place them over the top horizontal locking-bar guide and the next-to-bottom guide, since you'll need access to the bottoms of the tappets. Secure these with 2-56 screws. Don't glue them—the tappets or locking bars might need later fixing or adjusting.

Also add a bottom strip as a stop for the tappets. This should be one strip width (.312") from the bottom of the tappets' normal position. This provides a positive stop for the tappets at a width of one locking bar. Here's where I wish I would have made the base for the frame a bit longer—I had to add a small piece as an extension for the stop.

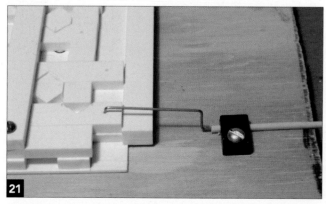

21

Actuating wire can be added to the ends of the tappets to control turnouts and signals directly.

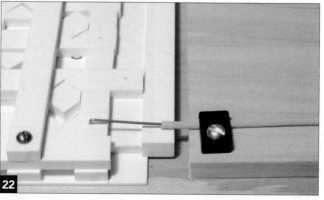

22

Mounting the actuating wire guide on a wood base eliminates the need to bend the actuating wire.

23

Slide switches can be mounted in holes or a gap in the plywood at the end of the frame. Each switch must line up with its tappet.

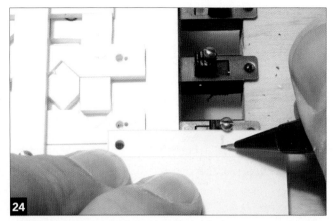

24

With tappet and switch reversed, mark the connecting strip at the left of the screw shaft to indicate the amount of throw needed.

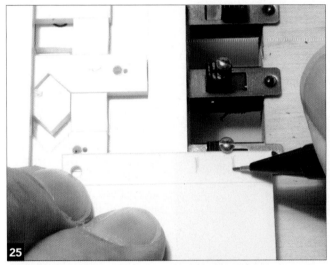

25

Move the tappet and switch to the normal positions, then mark the strip to the right of the screw head.

26

The connecting strip throws the slide switch as the tappet moves between normal and reversed positions.

Signals and turnout controls

You can use the motion from the tappets to control signals and turnouts in several ways. We'll look at a couple of them. No doubt you can come up with other methods as well.

Start by securing the locking bed to a piece of plywood. My locking frame measures about 5½" wide by 4¼" long, and its styrene base is 6" square. The size of the wood base will depend on how you will mount the frame to your layout.

You can use actuating wire to control turnouts and semaphore signals directly.

The Hump Yard levers include a length of actuating wire that's encased in a plastic sleeve, and it works very well for the job. You can see one way to connect this wire to the end of the tappets in **21**. Drill a hole the appropriate size in the end of the tappet to accept the wire, and clamp the wire guide near the end of the tappet.

Another option is shown in **22**, elevating the actuating wire connection to avoid the wire bends needed in the earlier installation.

You also can use the tappets to control electrical slide switches, which

then can be used to power turnouts or signals. I mounted the switches by mounting two pieces of plywood with a gap between them on a 1 x 2 frame, **23**. The switches sit in this gap and are nailed or screwed in place, aligned with the tappets.

The throw distance on the tappets matches the distance between the locking bars (.312"), which is longer than the throw on the DPDT microswitches that I used (Miniatronics no. 38-200-05). This will vary for you depending on the switches you use, but adjusting for this isn't difficult.

Use thin styrene or ABS strips (I cut .250"-wide strips from a scrap .040" styrene sheet) to transfer the motion from the tappets to the switches. Drill a no. 50 hole in the end of the tappet and tap it for a 2-56 screw; do the same in the top of each slide switch. Drill a no. 42 hole in one end of the connecting strip to clear the screw on the tappet end.

Start with tappet no. 1. Set the tappet in the reversed position and throw the slide switch away from the tappet. Place the connecting strip in the proper place on the tappet,

133

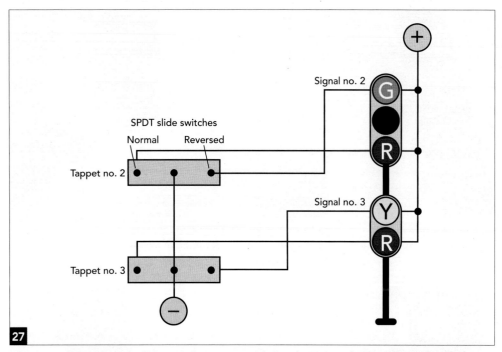

27

Here's one way of using slide switches to control signals. You can adapt them to various situations (such as having separate home and distant signals).

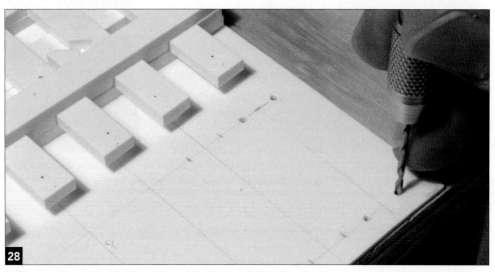

28

Drill mounting holes for the Hump Yard levers following the template in the instructions.

24, and mark the strip at the left edge of the screw shaft. This indicates the amount of throw needed. Next, move the tappet to the normal position and throw the slide switch toward the tappet. Mark the strip at the right edge of the screw shaft, **25**. This indicates how much motion is needed to pull the slide switch back toward the tappet.

Use these marks as a guide for cutting a notch in the connecting strip. Remove the screw from the switch, place the connecting strip in place, then attach it by adding the screws at each end, **26**.

You can use the slide switches to control signals directly, **27**. To control turnouts, follow wiring instructions for the make of switch machine you're using.

You also can combine mechanical and electrical control by connecting an actuating wire to the end of the connecting strip. For example, you can use the slide switch to control indicator lights on a control panel while using the actuating rod to mechanically throw a semaphore.

Connecting the levers

You now can place the whole machine in business by mounting the control levers in place. Many different approaches can be taken for assembling and mounting the Hump Yard levers (most of which are detailed in the product's instructions). You can mount the panel and locking bed vertically to save space, or you can do as I did and mount it flat. Once again, be creative and play with the various components.

Mounting on a flat surface requires the bottom of the lever to be trimmed and a new mounting hole drilled for the wire connector. The instructions include a template for drilling mounting holes. Drill these so each lever will be aligned with its tappet, **28**.

You'll need to connect the bottom of each lever to its tappet. I used .025" wire from the Hump Yard actuating wire. This wire must be heavy enough not to twist when moved. The amount of throw from a hole drilled at the bottom of the lever was just about perfect for the .312" width of the locking levers. You may have to adjust the shape of the wire depending upon your installation, **29**.

Test the lever with the wire to make sure it works properly. The lever must push the tappet all the way to the bumping strip when the lever is thrown. You can see two levers and wires installed in **30**. Cutting a gap in the spacer on the tappet side of the lever mounting base allows the wire to pass between the lever's mounting legs to the tappet.

As you design and build your machine, keep in mind that the arrangement of the levers and tappets from left to right will depend on the end of the tappets where the levers are located.

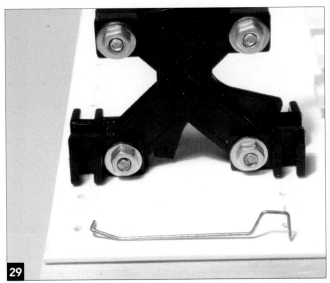

29

The bottom of the lever has been trimmed, and a new hole drilled for the wire. Shape the wire to match the tappet and lever.

30

The lever with connecting wire is attached to the tappet.

I originally had planned to have the levers to the rear of the locking bed, but it worked best for my installation to have the levers in front of the locking bed, **31**. This requires the tappets to be located in a mirror image compared to the original dog chart (or else your levers will be numbered from 8 to 1 from left to right).

This wasn't critical for this particular interlocking because it is symmetrical (levers 1 and 8 are mirror images of each other, as are 2 and 7, etc.). Thus, on my model, lever 8 became lever 1 and so on. Keep this in mind as you design and build your own machine.

Frame and track diagram

I covered the frame bed, **31**, while allowing the levers to come through a fake floor. The L-shaped side brackets are cut from ½" plywood. The dimensions aren't critical, and will vary depending upon your available space. The front and top surfaces are .040"

31

The frame is made of plywood. The L-shaped cover over the levers is sheet styrene, screwed in place to allow later access if needed for maintenance.

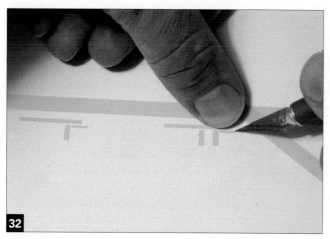

Use strips of thin masking tape to mark track and signal locations.

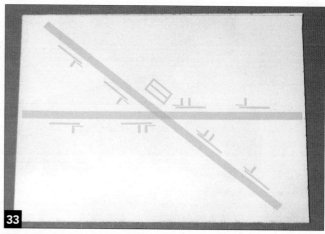

The masking tape is applied, and the board is ready for black paint.

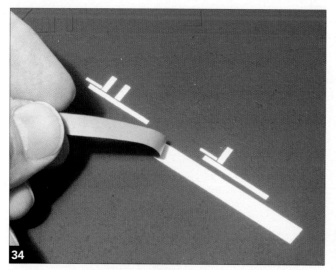

Peel the masking tape away to reveal the track diagram. Touch up any areas as needed with a brush.

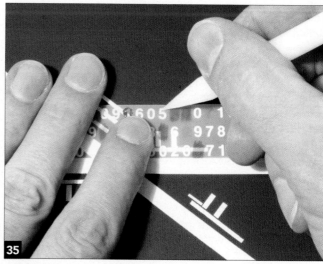

Dry transfers work well for marking signal numbers and any other lettering needed.

styrene, cut to fit, with a slot cut in the top to allow the levers to pass through. The styrene pieces are glued together to form an angle, and the completed piece is screwed to the frame to allow access to the mechanism.

The track diagram, also screwed in place on the frame, is essential to let operators know which levers correspond with each turnout and signal. These can be made in several different ways. I used the tried-and-true masking-tape-and-paint method, which has been popular for years in building control panels.

Thin (1⁄8") tempered hardboard, such as Masonite brand, works well for these, and heavy styrene will also work well. The overall size of the diagram can vary depending on the complexity of the diagram and how you choose to mount it. Start by painting the board white. Use strips of ¼" masking tape to mark the track location on the board. Next, use tape to mark the signal locations, **32**. This looks complex at first, but the process is simple and goes quickly.

I laid a strip of ¼"-wide masking tape on a piece of glass, then cut it in both

thick and thin segments to represent semaphore blades. The thick pieces mark the blades at their normal aspects, while the thin pieces show the blade position when reversed. Use more pieces of narrow (.080") tape to mark the outline of the interlocking tower location on the diagram. Photo **33** shows the masking in place. Make sure the tape is burnished firmly to the board so no paint leaks under it.

Paint the board a contrasting color. I used a spray can of flat black paint. Use light coats, making sure the board is completely

covered. Once the paint is dry, peel the masking tape off, **34**, and touch up any areas as needed.

Add numbers to the signals and turnouts using dry transfers, **35**. I used a lettering set from Woodland Scenics. Burnish the transfers firmly to the board, then remove the backing sheet.

As **1** shows, my board simply shows the track layout and numbers, but you can easily dress up your board by adding indicator lights to show the position of signals and turnouts or to show track occupancy. Mount the track plan to the frame, and your interlocking machine is complete.

You can use other methods to make track diagrams, including designing and printing them from a computer. This works well if you have a lot of lettering, artwork, and logos to include. You can also use colored pinstriping tape on backgrounds of various colors.

Designing dog charts

You can use the above methods to build other simple or complex interlocking machines. Here are a couple of other samples to get you going.

Figure **36** shows a simple junction with a branch line diverging from a main line, together with the dog chart for the junction. This interlocking has a single turnout and three possible routes. The three home signals are normally red-over-red, and the distant signals are normally at yellow. The home signals for trains entering at A and B have permanent lower red signals because only one route is possible. Lining the route for trains entering at A results in green-over-red (clear), while lining the route for trains entering at B gives a yellow-over-red (approach) aspect because it's a slow speed route.

For trains coming from C, lining the straight (normal) route to A provides green-over-red, while lining the slower speed route to B gives a red-over-yellow (diverging approach) aspect. You can change these aspects to match the desired speeds for your modeled routes.

The dog chart isn't much more complex than the earlier crossing, but

it does include a spring-loaded locking bar. Gordy Odegard's brass locking bed provides an example, **37**.

You can see the track plan for Gordy's original machine, with the dog chart, in **38**.

You can apply these charts and ideas to similar and more complex junctions. Start by writing a locking chart for all signals and switches, then carry the

pattern to the dog chart. In designing and building your own locking bed, you're bound to end up with a notch or two in the wrong place. Try to work through it, and keep playing with the lever combinations until the machine works properly.

CTC-style board

With the growing popularity of all-relay interlocking systems in the 1930s and

1940s, many junctions became controlled by panels of a similar style to Centralized Traffic Control dispatcher's panels. Boards such as the one in **39** are easy to build thanks to the nice plates and knobs offered by Rix Products (kit no. 628-61, **40**). These are molded in silver plastic and must be painted. The best way to do this is to paint them semi-gloss black (I

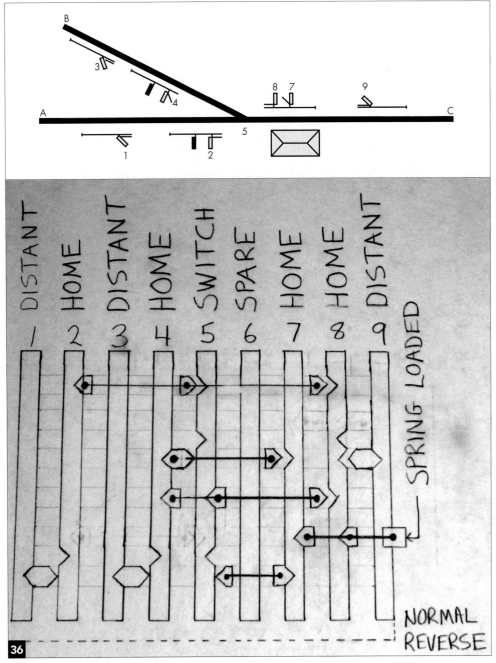

Here's a simple diverging (non-crossing) junction with its dog chart.

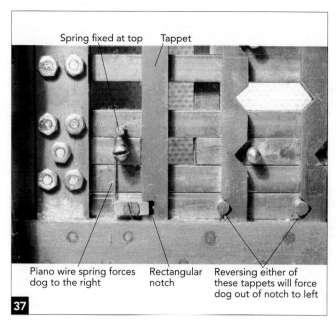

Spring fixed at top   Tappet

Piano wire spring forces dog to the right

Rectangular notch

Reversing either of these tappets will force dog out of notch to left

37

Some locking beds require spring-loaded locking bars.

used a spray can), then rub their faces on fine sandpaper. This neatly removes the paint from the raised letters and details as seen in **40**. Rix provides decals to use for numbering the plates.

Building a working interlocking is more complex with these components compared to the lever/mechanical plant. We'll look at controlling a junction, but without the actual interlocking mechanism. Many model railroaders have used computers to control interlockings of this type.

Start by planning your control panel. Its size will be determined by your available space and location as well as by the complexity of the trackwork and number of control switches needed.

As with the mechanical interlocking, you'll need to determine the number of signals, their locations, and the aspects desired. I followed the same basic plan as in **36**, but with a permanent yellow approach signal on the branch and approach signals on the main line that usually are at yellow and go to green when reversed, **41**.

With this type of machine, turnouts are given odd numbers and signals even numbers. Both are numbered from left to right. The turnout panel switches are in the top row; the bottom row is for signal switches.

For turnout switches, the N and R indicate normal and reversed positions (with corresponding red indicator lamps). The normal route of a turnout generally is shown on the track diagram with an unbroken line (straight on our model), with the reversed position indicated by a break in the line.

For the signal switches, L and R indicate that signals are cleared to the Left or Right, with corresponding green indicator lamps; when positioned in the middle, the red middle lamp is lit. Note that signals on the diagram are numbered with an L or R, indicating the direction of travel they govern.

Our model is simplified compared to the real thing. For example, a real panel would have a code button below the control switches that would actuate the switch settings. You can use one switch for each signal

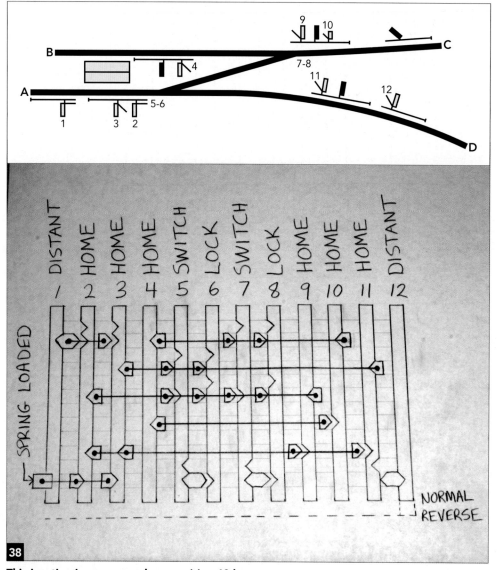

38

This junction is more complex, requiring 12 levers.

head; doing so makes the wiring easier but will also require more components and therefore more space on your fascia or control panel.

It's best if you can do as the prototype does: control two opposing signals with a common rotary switch, with the L and R indicating the route is cleared for travel toward the left or right per the track diagram. For example, on our sample the signal 4 switch aligns the opposing home signals for the straight route, and the signal 6 switch aligns the opposing home signals for the diverging route.

As the photos show, if a control switch sets a signal for one direction only (as with distant signals 2R and 8L), then only one directional indicator lamp is needed.

Building the panel

Figure **42** shows the full-sized template I made on a pad of drawing paper for marking the center points of the mounting holes for the rotary switches and panel indicator lights. The dimensions I used for spacing switches next to each other are shown in **43**. I used tempered hardboard for my panel; you can also use thin plywood or other thin material.

Tape the template in place over the panel, then transfer the markings to the board by poking through the template with an awl or scriber.

Drill mounting holes for each component. Your hole dimensions will depend upon the shaft size of your rotary switches (3/8" is common) and lamps (I used bulbs from Radio Shack that required 1/2" holes). A spade bit works best for drilling hardboard,

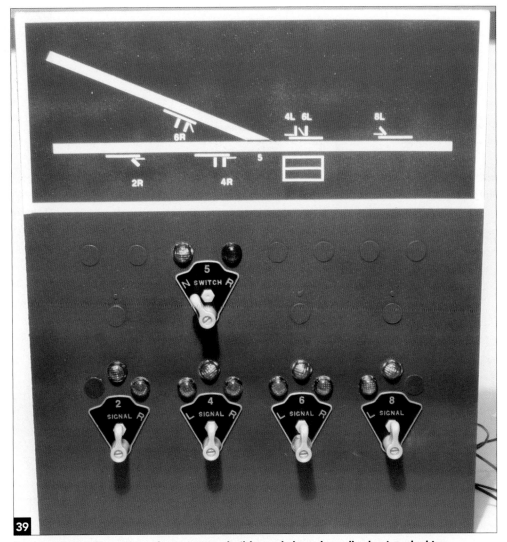

39

Panel switches from Rix make it easy to build panels based on all-relay interlocking machines.

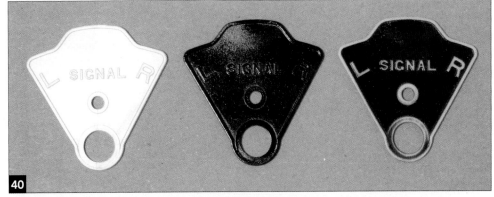

40

The Rix plates are molded in silver plastic (left). Painting them black (middle) and then sanding the letters and trim gives a realistic appearance.

as its design will cut the material cleanly without pulling material out, as a regular spiral bit tends to do.

Prototype panels had small knockout disks

covering unused holes. To simulate these, add disks of 1/2"-diameter, .020" styrene to the unused switch and lamp positions. Use cyanoacrylate (CA) to glue them in place.

Assembly

I used the same masking tape technique as with the board in **1**. I painted my panel dark green—a common color for these

139

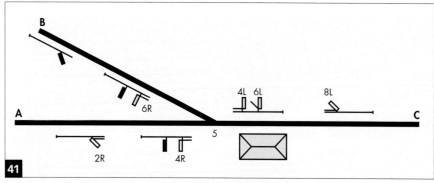

41

Here's the signal labeling for the junction panel in 39.

44

The Rix knob fits nicely over the D-shaped knob of the rotary switch.

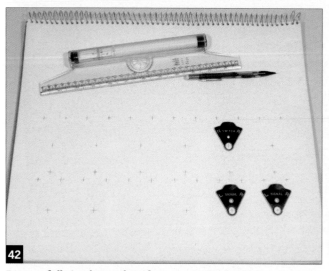

42

Draw a full-sized template for your control panel.

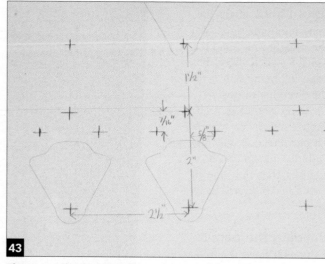

43

These are the spacing dimensions used for the components.

panels—using a spray can.

The indicator lamps are ½"-mount, 12-volt bulbs from Radio Shack (nos. 272-332 red, 272-337A green). They work perfectly for these panels and would work for many other projects as well. Simply push them into place on the panel; the sprung side clips on their housings will hold them in place.

I used CA to glue the Rix switch plates in position, although the rotary switches will hold them securely once they're installed. The photos show a two-pole, six-position rotary switch with a 3⁄8" mount and D-shaped shaft, **44**.

A 2P6T (two-pole, six-throw) rotary will control the signals, but to get the

indicator lamps operating off the same switch you'll need a rotary with two layers (or wafers), **45**. Use non-shorting rotary switches with 30-degree spacing contacts.

Wiring will depend on the signals you're using. If you're using a type of color light signals with LEDs or bulbs, follow the diagram in **45**. That diagram shows how signal switch 4 and signals 4R and 4L are wired. The voltage used will depend on the type of LED or bulb you're using. Note that polarity must be correct when using LEDs, and you'll need to use appropriate resistors.

You can modify the circuits to control switch machines, signal drivers,

and other accessories. You also can simplify any of the above controls and simply use slide, toggle, or rotary switches to control turnouts and signals. Figure **46** shows some simplified control circuits, and the following section shows how to actuate a semaphore with a slow-motion switch machine.

Semaphore control

For realistic operation, semaphore blades should move slowly. The following instructions from Jeff Scherb show how it can be done. A slow-motion switch motor can provide the animation, but these switch motors generally only have two positions, and this type of semaphore needs three. Fortunately, Circuitron's

Tortoise switch motor can easily be wired to have the needed third (center) position.

Circuitron produces a remote signal-actuator mounting bracket and vertical motion mechanism that adapts Tortoise switch machines to operate semaphore signals, but it's not hard to make your own drive mechanism—here's how Jeff did it, **47**.

An actuating lever is made from .025" x ¼" brass strip. A 4-40 screw through a hole in one end of the lever attaches the lever to the Tortoise actuator. A "T" nut secured to the Tortoise casing and another screw provide the pivot point for the lever. Several 1⁄16" holes drilled

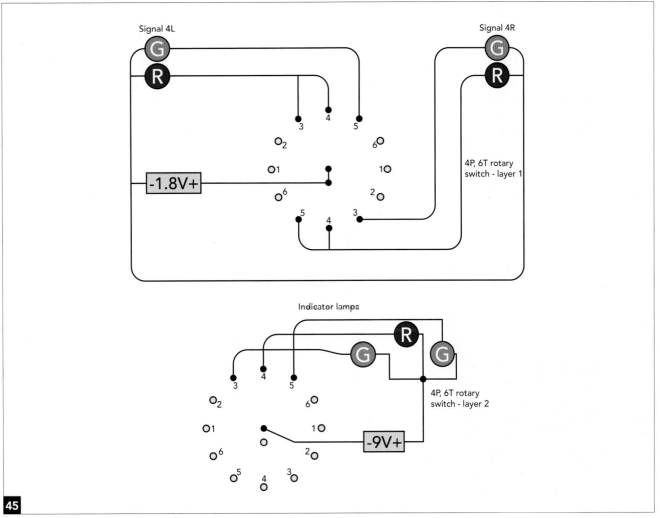

45

A 2P6T rotary switch with two wafers controls both panel lights and signals.

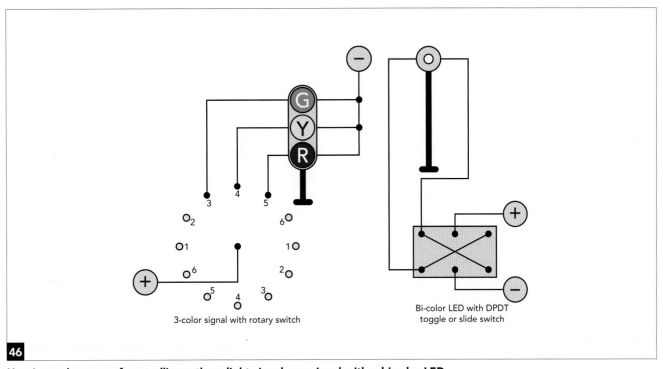

3-color signal with rotary switch

Bi-color LED with DPDT
toggle or slide switch

46

Here's another way of controlling a three-light signal or a signal with a bi-color LED.

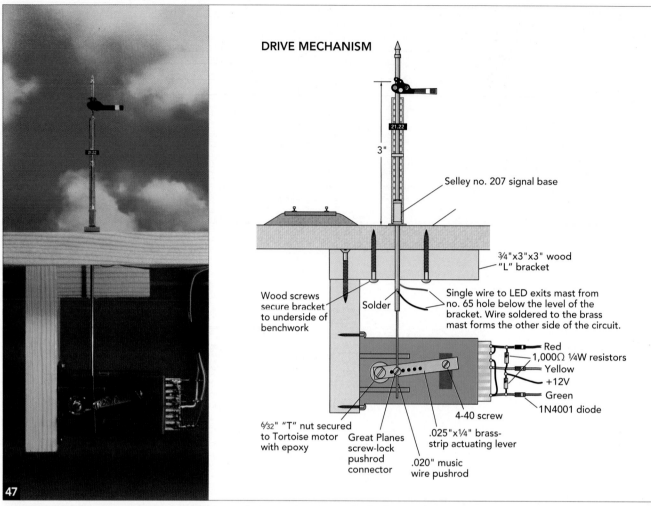

DRIVE MECHANISM

3"

Selley no. 207 signal base

¾"x3"x3" wood "L" bracket

Wood screws secure bracket to underside of benchwork

Solder

Single wire to LED exits mast from no. 65 hole below the level of the bracket. Wire soldered to the brass mast forms the other side of the circuit.

Red
1,000Ω ¼W resistors
Yellow
+12V
Green
1N4001 diode

4-40 screw

%₃₂" "T" nut secured to Tortoise motor with epoxy

Great Planes screw-lock pushrod connector

.020" music wire pushrod

.025"x¼" brass-strip actuating lever

Jeff Scherb built this mechanism for driving a three-position semaphore using a Tortoise switch machine.

through the lever provide a range of adjustment for setting the proper distance of motion. A Great Planes GPMQ3870 screw-lock pushrod connector provides the anchor on the actuating lever for the blade pushrod.

To mount the Tortoise under the layout, make an "L" bracket from ¾" pine. Dimensions for this bracket will depend on whatever obstructions you need to clear under the layout.

The wiring is quite simple, and requires only two resistors and three diodes. When the green input is grounded, current flows from +12V through R2 to the motor to ground. When the red input is grounded, current flows

from +12V through R1 to the motor to ground. When the yellow input is grounded, current flows through R1 or R2 and the SPDT switches depending on the current position of the switch motor, but the motion always will be toward the center. When the switch breaks contact in the center of travel, the motor will stop, giving us the center position.

Diodes D1, D2, and D3 prevent reverse voltages from flowing back through the motor and into the signal logic circuit. This wiring should be compatible with any three-color-signal logic circuit that provides a grounded output. Any circuit that has outputs for red, yellow, and green, where

each output goes to ground to light its light, should work just fine.

The color-light circuit Jeff Scherb presented in "Simple circuits for automatic block signals" in the March 2001 *Model Railroader* can be used with semaphores. To use that circuit, resistors R1, R4, and R6 should be 470Ω, ½W, and the supply voltage should be 12 volts to provide proper drive for the Tortoise.

Also, using that circuit means you can mix and match semaphores with color-light and searchlight signals in the same system. To complete the wiring, a 1KΩ, ¼W resistor should be wired in series with the white LED to limit the current to safe levels for the LED.

Even if you don't have the electronics for a signal system, you can install semaphore signals and wire them to be operated manually. A three-position rotary switch can be used to connect each of the green, yellow, and red terminals of the semaphore circuit to ground.

Glossary

ABS: Automatic Block Signal System

Absolute Signal: A signal that when indicating Stop cannot be passed by a train without permission to pass being granted by a dispatcher or operator, or by following specific rules to provide for safe movement of trains.

APB: Absolute-Permissive Block Signal System

Automatic Signal: A signal not controlled by a human that responds only to track conditions ahead. An Automatic Signal, as long as it is not also an Absolute Signal, can in most cases be passed by a train even when it displays a red aspect. Typically, the train must first stop before proceeding, then proceed only at restricted speed (i.e., not exceeding 20 mph, and able to stop in one-half the distance of vision short of any train, car, open switch, track machine, or person, watching out for broken rails).

Block Signal: Any signal that governs speed or grants authority to enter the track beyond the signal.

Controlled signal: A signal controlled by a human (e.g., dispatcher or operator), to govern route or priority of traffic, that grants authority to a train to enter the track beyond the signal. Controlled signals are almost always Absolute Signals.

CTC: Centralized Traffic Control

Dispatcher: the railroad employee responsible for safe and efficient train movement over a specific territory.

Fixed signal: A signal that displays only one aspect, permanently.

Head: The part of the signal displaying the aspect—the part with the semaphore or light. Heads may be mounted on masts, on bridges, on cantilever arms, or on the ground.

Home signals: Absolute signals controlled by the dispatcher or the operator that mark the entrance to an interlocking and govern movements on each track entering the interlocking. Home signals grant authority to move to the next controlled signal, which may be hundreds of feet or miles away. The term "home signal" is also commonly used to describe the signal facing the entrance to a siding.

Interlocking limits: the on-track boundaries of an individual interlocking plant.

Interlocking plant: The general area of an interlocking including all switches, derails, moveable bridges, signals, and other elements between and including the signals governing entrance into the area.

Interlocking signals: Home signals, or other controlled signals within the interlocking, but not at the entrance.

Nameplate or Numberplate: A fixed metal plate displaying some combination of numbers and/or letters mounted on a signal and considered part of the aspect of the signal.

Normal: the description of a turnout aligned for the most frequent movement, typically straight-ahead moves.

Operator: a railroad employee responsible to line the routes at the direction of the dispatcher (he or she is said to "operate the interlocking plant"). Traditionally, operators were located in interlocking towers but modern systems can move the operator to remote locations.

Reverse: the description of a turnout aligned for the less frequent movement, usually for diverging moves.

Searchlight: A type of signal head that uses a single lamp and a moving mechanism to change the displayed color.

Signal: one or more lights or semaphore arms (the "Head") and any attached nameplates or numberplates that are arranged in such a manner as to convey a signal aspect.

Signal aspect: an arrangement of lights or semaphore arms that, in conjunction with the owning railroad's rules, communicates information regarding speed and/or route related to the track ahead. Aspects are what the signal looks like to the viewer. Remember: Aspects are Appearance.

Signal indication: the railroad rules describing movement regulations and restrictions associated with a particular signal aspect. Indications are the information conveyed by the signal aspect. Remember: Indications are Information.

Bibliography

Books

Classic Railway Signal Tower, The by Stephen A. McEvoy. Stephen A. McEvoy and Instant Publisher, 2007

Railroad Signaling by Brian Solomon. Voyageur Press, 2010

Triumph I—Altoona to Pitcairn by Charles S. Roberts and David Messier. Barnard, Roberts and Co., Baltimore, Md., 1997

Periodicals

"D&RGW Expedites Trains With Centralized Control" *Railway Signaling*, November 1929 Vol. 22, No. 11, pp 414-416.

"Impatient pioneer of 1851 Honored" by Richard J. H. Johnston. New York *Times*, September 22 1951.

"Model mechanical interlockings" by Bill Darnaby, *Model Railroader*, January 2004, p. 122-128

"A signal system to fit any railroad" by Bruce Carpenter, MR, April 2017

Websites

multimodalways.org

Notes on Pennsylvania Railroad Operation and Signaling: mysite. du.edu/~jcalvert/railway/prr/prrsig.htm

onondagacutoff.blogspot.com

Prototype info: jonroma.net

Railways: History, Signalling, Engineering: mysite.du.edu/~jcalvert/ railway/railhom.htm#aspect

wiringfordcc.com by Allan Gartner

Integrated Signal Systems: integratedsignalsystems.com

NCE Corp. ncedcc.com

Digitrax: digitrax.com

RR-CirKits: rr-cirkits.com

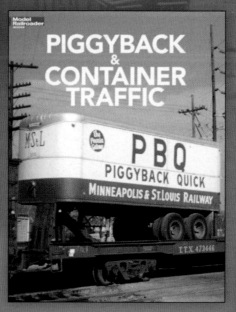
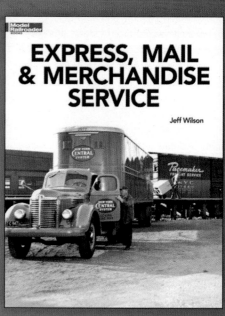